CHRISTMAS
FROM OBER

ELMFIELD RUDOLF STEINER SCHOOL LTD.
LOVE LANE
STOURBRIDGE
WEST MIDLANDS
DY8 2EA
TEL: 01384 394633
CHARITY No: 527521

CHRISTMAS PLAYS
FROM OBERUFER

The Paradise Play—The Shepherds Play—The Kings Play

Translated by A.C. Harwood
Edited by Hélène Jacquet

Sophia Books

Sophia Books
Hillside House, The Square
Forest Row, RH18 5ES

www.rudolfsteinerpress.com

Published by Sophia Books 2007
An imprint of Rudolf Steiner Press

First published in English in earlier versions in 1944, 1961, 1973 and 1993

© Rudolf Steiner Press 2007

The moral right of the author has been asserted under the Copyright, Designs and Patents Act, 1988

All rights reserved. No part of this publication may be reproduced, stored in a retrieval system, or transmitted, in any form or by any means, electronic, mechanical, photocopying or otherwise, without the prior permission of the publishers

A catalogue record for this book is available from the British Library

ISBN 978 185584 184 0

Cover by Andrew Morgan Design
Typeset by DP Photosetting, Neath, West Glamorgan
Printed and bound in Great Britain by Cromwell Press Limited, Trowbridge, Wiltshire

Dedicated to the first actors of these plays in England: the teachers of Michael Hall School, Sussex

CONTENTS

Translator's Preface   1
Editor's Introduction   5
Director's Notes   9
Costume Indications   13
Make-up Indications   17

THE PLAYS
Paradise Play   19
Shepherds Play   43
Kings Play   79

COLOUR PLATES
Costume Indications   *after* p. 120

TRANSLATOR'S PREFACE

The Plays here translated were collected in the forties of the nineteenth century by Karl Julius Schröer—the friend and teacher of Rudolf Steiner—from the little island of Oberufer on the Danube near Pressburg, close to the frontiers of Austria and Hungary. Some time in the sixteenth or early seventeenth century a group of German people had migrated there from the neighbourhood of Lake Constance and had taken with them the cycle of religious plays which they had received by tradition from their ancestors. When Schröer collected the plays, the parts were still hereditary in certain families; no complete copy existed but each family treasured a manuscript of the words of one particular part. Surrounded as they were by people of a different nation and speaking a different language, the peasants of Oberufer preserved unaltered, in a way found in no other similar German plays, both the text itself and the tradition of acting.

The preparation for the Plays and the manner of acting have been thus described by Rudolf Steiner, who received the account from Schröer himself. In the autumn, after harvest, the peasants who were to take part met together and rehearsals began. All parts were played by men, as in the Elizabethan theatre, and during the time of rehearsal all members of the cast had to lead—as far as they could—a moral and respectable life, abstaining alike from visits to alehouses and from the singing of bawdy songs. Before the actual performance the whole company went in procession through the village. They were headed by the 'Tree-singer', who carried in his hand the small 'Paradise Tree'—a kind of symbol of the Tree of Life—and the rear was brought up by the 'Star-singer', who bore a golden star on the end of multiple wooden scissors—a larger version of a familiar children's toy—which could shoot the star over the other actors and hold it aloft over the head of Mary. On reaching the inn where the performance was to take place, the company went in to dress, with the exceptions of the Angel, who stayed outside, and the Devil, who ran riot through the town, blowing a cowhorn and driving everyone he could into the inn to see the performance. Once in the inn the audience arranged itself in a horseshoe and the performance began, the Tree-singer acting as prologue to the *Paradise Play* and the Star-singer to the *Shepherds Play*. After these two plays, of which the *Paradise Play* was acted second, a third satirical comedy—somewhat in the Greek fashion—was added, in which, however, the actors who had played the Holy Characters were not allowed to take part. The *Play of the Three Kings* was acted at another time and under somewhat different circumstances, being in closer connection with the church. The *Paradise Play* and *Shepherds Nativity Play*, however, were always associated together, for in the Middle Ages they still knew what modern man has forgotten, that there is no meaning in the Redemption without the Fall, and that

> Had not the apple taken been
>   The apple taken been
> Then had never our Lady,
>   A-been Heaven's Queen.

The form of the Plays seems to point to the very origin of drama. The actors, or singers as they were called, sing a song in procession, after which the characters concerned come forward and act what has just been sung, while the rest of the company seat themselves at the back or side of the stage. This ancient form is especially marked in the case of the *Paradise Play*, which is really one long ballad interspersed with dramatic scenes. The Devil acts as scene-shifter in the *Paradise Play*; and the Devil for Herod, and the Page for the Kings in the *Three Kings Play*. Traditionally, the Angel in the *Shepherds Play* carries a star on a staff, and the Angel in the *Kings Play* has a picture of Mother and Child beneath the star.

TRANSLATOR'S PREFACE

A word may be added about the translation. When there is much wonderful poetry in such old English plays as the *Coventry Plays*, it may seem superfluous to translate Christmas Plays from another tongue. Experience has shown, however, that these particular plays, which are both more childlike and more dramatic than the old English plays, make a deeper impression on children than any other old plays available. For a dreadful alternative waits on the would-be-writer of modern Nativity Plays. To make the thing realistic, and convince the audience that it really did happen and a real baby was born in a real stable, he has to introduce language from a life with so different an idiom that it falsifies the picture of the birth of a child in an age when the bearing of children was treated both more simply and more spiritually than it is today. Or he may treat the theme poetically, with the almost inevitable consequence of reducing the matter to a beautiful dream, in which idealized shepherds salute a symbolic child. The life of the Middle Ages, however, was still sufficiently akin to the time of the Birth of Christ for the Nativity to be represented in its own language and forms.

The original plays are in dialect and lose enormously in vigour and colour in any non-dialect translation. Unfortunately, most modern English people have been robbed of their birthright of a dialect, and, being myself one of those unfortunates, I have been forced to put the translation into a kind of biblical English with some deliberate archaisms. I hope that readers will find the language on the right side of Wardour Street. But the plays are not meant to be read, and in actual performance the translation has stood the test of a good many annual performances. The two Prologues probably form the least satisfactory part. They can either be omitted, or provide the basis for such local pleasantries as may suit the particular performance.

The music composed by Leopold van der Pals on the basis of the original folk melodies may be procured through the publishers of this translation.

For this English version music has also been composed by Dr Brien Masters, to whom enquiries should be addressed at Michael Hall, Kidbrooke Park, Forest Row, Sussex.

A.C.H.

EDITOR'S INTRODUCTION

Having produced, watched, performed in, studied and researched the Christmas Plays from Oberufer for over 45 years, my husband and I have often been asked by colleagues how to produce them. It is hoped that the practical indications added to this new edition will help those who face this task.

The plays have now developed a tradition based on indications given by Rudolf Steiner when producing the plays in Dornach in the first decades of the twentieth century and which were written down by Else Klevers with the help of Marie Steiner. These should not be viewed as a hindrance to the director's creativity but rather as a help to understand the deep meaning of the plays, which Rudolf Steiner took the trouble and time to produce and introduce at every performance. In an address given on 30 December 1917 he said:

> One may say, indeed, that these plays belong to those things which have unfortunately been lost, have disappeared, and which one so gladly, so gladly, would like to have afresh. For they are indeed such as if, through them, one reminded oneself of what is connected so intimately with the being of one's spiritual life.

In Oberufer's time the plays were done in a *very* different manner. They were all performed on the same day from 3 o'clock onwards. If in the evening there were still a few enthusiastic spectators left in their seats, then the plays began again. This sometimes went on until the small hours until the very last guest had gone. Oddly enough, the performance started with the *Nativity Play* (*Shepherds Play*), followed by the *Paradise Play* and concluded with a *Carnival Play* ('The Shoemaker and the Tailor'), thus continuing the ancient tradition of the Satyr players.

The plays were performed in a tavern, the acting being done in the central corridor. The spectators sat on benches, on either side and at one end of the room. The fourth side was curtained off and was used as a changing room and entrance for everyone. The choral procession of the company went along the walls which surrounded the spectators. The only props were a stool for Mary, a little stable carried by Joseph, and, for the Tree-singer, a man-sized juniper tree. The greeting of the Tree-singer was a real one: each person, when greeted, stood up and raised his hat, as did the 'whole worshipping town'!

The text of plays was not spoken but chanted in medieval singsong. The chanting players walked up and down the aforementioned passage taking four big strong steps in one direction, then, on the fourth step, turning and going in the opposite direction. Those players who were not playing at any one time sat on a bench. In addition to the chanting were the songs proper, usually carols such as *Vom Himmel Hoch*.

It is clear that with his new productions, Rudolf Steiner gave a new lease of life to these plays and planted them firmly in our time.

Milenko Kaukler researched the history of the plays and wrote:

> Schröer's texts of these plays were significantly improved in four ways by Rudolf Steiner. First, he separated the *Nativity Play* from the *Kings Play*, which over the course of the centuries had been intermingled. Secondly, he recreated lost passages such as the part of the Tree-singer in the *Paradise Play* and the Shepherd's supper scene. Thirdly, he began to correct corrupt and meaningless passages. Finally, Steiner adapted the awkwardly artificial language of the plays (which in the Oberufer text remains very close to Luther's 'Hochdeutsch'—'High German'—and shows only the strong influence of village dialects) to the dialect of Oberufer, particularly in the more folksy parts. As an Austrian he could do that.

The Oberufer plays are performed in many languages and in many schools, homes, anthroposophical institutions, etc., totalling far in excess of 500 performances each year. This makes these plays probably among some of the most performed in the world.

A.C. Harwood, a poet in his own right (*The Voice of Cecil Harwood*, Rudolf Steiner Press) gave the English-speaking world an excellent translation of the plays, with beautiful rhythms and an exquisite language. Yet, when asked, he willingly changed a few lines and added one to help give the exact meaning of the original play; these have now been included in this edition. Some lines were changed in the four different editions, and in this latest one I have used the text most performed at Michael Hall. Finally, in the German publication the order of the *Shepherds Play* is the following: song, Angel's speech, song, Annunciation, song, the Journey to Bethlehem. For the sake of clarity and the time-span involved this order was already changed in the very first edition of the English text, hence following the text of the original publication by J. Schröer (Keck und Compagnie, Vienna 1858). In Germany, to accompany the plays, the music by Van der Pals is mostly performed. Here we use music by Brian Masters, a talented musician and composer who gave us a music well tailored to our times.

To do justice to the plays, they should be acted without pathos, in a dignified way and with simple humour. Heinz Muller in *Spuren auf dem Weg* (Mellinger Verlag, Stuttgart) recalls:

> And the masterly thing that the Tree-singer has to create is that purely through the words, disciplines and gestures he must make everything living. With Rudolf Steiner the work became living just through the peasant style of the performance; the word become spirit under his powerful creation.

And further:

Shortly before the *Paradise Play* performance, the Tree-singer came to Rudolf Steiner and said: 'Oh Herr Doctor, I have had a complete blackout; the earth seems to give away under my feet.' Rudolf Steiner put his hand firmly on the actor's back and, saying 'Nonsense! You are as fit as a fiddle,' he gave him a tremendous push and the Tree-singer found himself on stage and the play began.

The plates giving an impression of costume designs, based on Rudolf Steiner's directions, were painted by the Editor's father, Eugen Witta, who saw the plays produced by Rudolf Steiner many times while working as a young architect on the first Goetheanum. He later produced the plays for many years in France.

Hélène Jacquet

But if in aught we have gone astray
And shown your worships what was not fit
Blame not our will, but our lack of wit
Think it, but well, so all's made right—
And we wish you from God Almighty, Good Night

DIRECTOR'S NOTES

1. *Stage Settings*
In the *Paradise Play* the large Christmas tree is placed stage left, from the Audience, two-thirds of the way upstage, with shiny red apples hanging from the branches—the flaming sword and chain are hidden behind. God's throne, with a high rounded back, is covered with a white sheet and stands opposite the tree at stage right. Blue stage curtains.

In the *Shepherds Play* the Christmas tree, bearing 33 red roses and the signs representing the Evolution of Humanity (see diagram p. 11), stands in the same place as in the *Paradise Play*. Under the tree stands the rocking crib and Mary's stool. Behind the tree the shepherds' presents are hidden: wool, flour, bottle of milk and a lamb, ready to be picked up. Blue stage curtains.

In the *Kings Play* the stage is bare except for three benches. *Bench 1* along the wings stage right where the Angel, Mary, Joseph, Three Kings, Viligratia and Page sit. *Bench 2*—Herod, Lackey, Captain and Soldier sit on a bench along the back curtain, at right angles to Bench 1. *Bench 3*—the Three Priests and the Devil sit on a smaller bench also along the back curtain next to Herod's, so that when the Priests return after their scene they can upset the bench and let it fall. Mary's stool is fetched by the Page, from upstage right corner. The stool for the Kings: if fetched by the Page, from the upstage right corner; if fetched by the Devil, upstage left corner. White stage curtains.

2. *Processional Songs*
All the songs are marched in step so that the first beat of the bar falls on the right foot.

In the *Paradise Play* the company walks clockwise.

In the *Shepherds Play* the company walks clockwise until

the Child is born, then the direction is changed to indicate the change that occurred at that time in the evolution of humanity, and the company walks anticlockwise.

In the *Kings Play* the company walks anticlockwise.

3. Angel
The Angel walks always forwards—walking backwards shows one taking something back or getting away from a situation. The Angel, a messenger, always brings/gives something and does not take away.

4. Gestures
Rudolf Steiner mentioned that any gesture should always precede the words.

5. Use of Devil/Page
When Rudolf Steiner produced the *Kings Play* in Dornach he used the Devil to bring the Three Kings' stool, describing him as a 'stage-hand'. Subsequently, when the plays were produced in the schools, the Page performed that task.

6. Devil's Wings
In the *Paradise Play* the Devil wears wings but in the *Kings Play* he has no wings, except at the end when, summoned by the Angel, he comes to fetch Herod.

7. Bows
The Angel should bow three times every time. (In schools, because children may become restless, the Angel bows only once.)

8. Style and Settings
Each play starts in a different fashion.

The *Paradise Play* is the Will play depicting the beginning of mankind, and therefore also the 'Epic' play. Note that the songs interrupt the action at crucial points and preview or review it. The players come on stage from the wings, the most mysterious, unknown place for the audience. The company leaves at the end of the play through the audience, making the play part of our history.

The *Shepherds Play*, the Feeling, 'Lyric' play, speaks of human situations, present ones as well, and the human qualities necessary to cope with them. The players start from the audience and leave through the audience. The play is us, with what qualities we have acquired through the development of humanity.

The *Kings Play*, the Thinking play, is the play of our future starting now. It is the 'Dramatic' play where the challenge is to decide consciously what is right or wrong; where, before

The symbols and their position for the tree in the Shepherds Play

each action, there is a choice, and consequences after. The players start on the stage (not in the wings!) and finish on the stage, leaving a picture for our reflection.

Rudolf Steiner indicated that in each play the Angel should speak with a leaning towards its styles = Epic, Lyric, Dramatic.

9. *Shepherds' Gloves*
In the *Shepherds Play*, when the shepherds eat and drink the taking back of the gloves is essential. The rest can be left to the shepherds' imagination as long as the mood is jolly but not caricatural.

10. *Songs*
Both in the *Paradise Play* and *Shepherds Play* the songs tell the story of the next scene and the essential element of the play—the eating of the apple and birth of the Child. After the event the song recalls what has happened just before.

COSTUME INDICATIONS

(Variations of these can of course be made but the colours should be as far as possible the same—see Plates.)

PARADISE PLAY
TREE-SINGER: Green tunic. Red scarf. Dark trousers. Fur hat. Shepherd's criss-cross leggings. Carries a small Christmas tree with roots, decorated with red ribbons.
ANGEL: White dress and white wings. A plain gold band. (Soft gold should be used for all 'good' characters.) Gold ribbons criss-crossing the chest and a gold belt. The sword used should look like a flame. White socks/eurythmy shoes.
GOD: Light turquoise/blue dress. Dark red sash hanging from his left shoulder down across his chest and fastened on his right hip. Turquoise socks/eurythmy shoes.
EVA: Off-white dress (only the Angel should wear pure white) and belt. White socks/eurythmy shoes.
ADAM: Beige dress with darkish red stole and wide belt (forming a cross). Brown gauze veil covers him completely at the beginning of the play. Rib hidden in the fold of the dress. Beige socks/eurythmy shoes.
DEVIL: Black tunic and black wings. Black tights. Red frizzy wig with black horns. Black eurythmy shoes.

SHEPHERDS PLAY
ANGEL: Same as in the *Paradise Play*, but with a gold headband with a five-pointed star and/or a long, orange cloak fastened on the chest with a gold pentagram like a brooch, and just a gold belt. He carries a staff with a gold five-pointed star.
MARY: Cherry-red dress and cord. Long blue heavy veil covering the head, which is fastened at the wrists and open in front. Red socks/eurythmy shoes.

JOSEPH (older man): Brown dress. Blue sash (lighter blue than Mary's veil) hanging from his right shoulder across his chest and fastened on the left hip. Brown socks/eurythmy shoes. He carries a thick staff.
STAR-SINGER: Same as Tree-singer but blue tunic. He carries some wooden 'scissors' with a five-pointed star at the end, which can be extended so that the star stays over Mary's head during the walk through the audience, but not when the company is on the stage.
GALLUS: Blue tunic. Red scarf. Fur hat. Dark trousers. Criss-cross leggings. A three-quarter sleeveless fur or woollen coat fastened by a rope. He carries a shepherd's crook.
HUCKLE: Same as Gallus but red tunic and green scarf. At the beginning of the play he wears gloves.
MUCKLE: Same as Gallus but green tunic and light yellow scarf. Hat is of a lighter colour fur. He carries a bag for the Shepherd's food on his shoulder.
CRISPIN: Same as Gallus but a beige tunic and blue scarf. His sleeveless coat is lighter in colour and bigger (he is the richest shepherd).
INNKEEPERS: Wear traditional folk costumes—waistcoats, breeches, off-white blouses or shirts, scarves and aprons. On the head caps with tassels or scarves for women. Costume mainly black for Rufinus, mainly red/rust for Servilus and mainly brown for Titus. White socks and normal boots or black shoes in keeping with the style of the costumes. Titus carries a lantern.

KINGS PLAY
ANGEL: Same as in the *Shepherds Play*, but with a six-pointed star on the headband and/or can wear a long, very light yellow cloak fastened with a hexagram, like a brooch, on the chest and a gold belt. He carries a staff with the picture of Mary and the Child standing on a silver moon crescent, and a six-pointed star above Mary's head.
MARY: Same as in the *Shepherds Play* but with a thin silver crown.

COSTUME INDICATIONS

JOSEPH (a younger man than in the *Shepherds Play*): Same as in the *Shepherds Play*.

BALTHAZZAR: Off-white dress. Deep blue stole and small, deep blue mantle from the collar, just covering the shoulders. A crown with triangular points of the same blue. (The stole, crown and mantle form a cross.) He carries a sceptre. The gift can be a golden box or a flat bowl. White socks/eurythmy shoes.

MELCHIOR: Same as Balthazzar, but in red.

CASPAR: Same as Balthazzar, but in green.

PAGE: Blue tunic. Blue tights. Light yellow stole. Thin, light yellow ribbon for the headband. Blue eurythmy shoes.

VILIGRATIA: Purple dress and belt. A black mitre on his head with a golden design. Purple socks/eurythmy shoes. He carries a very big old book with powder in it to make the eventual cloud of dust when he shuts it.

HEROD: Black three-quarter length tunic and a belt with a gold button. Bright red three-quarter length coat. Black tights and traditional black shoes with golden buckle. (The gold for the bad characters should be metallic and very shiny.) He carries a golden sceptre. A golden chain of office. A golden crown with square indentations.

LACKEY: Dark crimson three-quarter length tunic. Grey tights. Silver belt.

CAPTAIN: Same tunic and belt as the Lackey (the tunic is covered with chain mail). A long dark red cloak fastened with silver brooches on each shoulder. Red tights. Boots or traditional black shoes. Steel helmet. When given it by the Devil, he carries a silver sword with the hilt in the shape of a cross.

SOLDIER: Same tunic and belt as the Lackey but black tights. Grey stole. Boots or traditional black shoes. Steel helmet. He carries a silver scimitar.

CAIAPHAS: White frizzy hair and beard. Grey dress with buttons in front, from top to bottom. Black belt. Black hat. Black socks/eurythmy shoes. Carries a scroll in his belt.

PILATE: Same as Caiaphas but grey hair and beard.

JONAS: Same as Caiaphas but ginger hair and beard.
JUDAS: Black dress and belt. Black scalp cap. Black socks/ eurythmy shoes.
DEVIL: Same as in the *Paradise Play*, but with a black frizzy wig with red horns. *No* wings until the *final* scene.

MAKE-UP INDICATIONS

PARADISE PLAY
ANGEL: See indication for the make-up of the eyes on Plate 7.
GOD: A blue triangle on the forehead, apex up. Long off-white hair, moustache and beard.
DEVIL: Strongly dark coloured make-up with a black triangle on the chin apex down. Red frizzy wig. Black horns.

SHEPHERDS PLAY
ANGEL: See indication for the make-up of the eyes on Plate 7.
JOSEPH: Grey hair and beard.
STAR-SINGER: Ruddy complexion.
GALLUS/HUCKLE: Ruddy complexion. Clean-shaven.
MUCKLE: Ruddy complexion. Grey hair and beard.
CRISPIN: Ruddy complexion. White hair and beard.

KINGS PLAY
ANGEL: See indications for the make-up of the eyes on Plate 7.
JOSEPH: Brown hair (and beard if wished).
BALTHAZZAR: Asian complexion. White hair.
MELCHIOR: Caucasian complexion. Blond/brown hair.
CASPAR: African complexion. Black hair.
VILIGRATIA: White hair and beard.
HEROD: Heavy eyebrows. Black hair.
CAIAPHAS: Frizzy white hair and beard.
PILATE: Frizzy grey hair and beard.
JONAS: Frizzy ginger hair and beard.
DEVIL: Same as in the *Paradise Play*, but with a frizzy black wig. Red horns.

ANGELS' EYEBROWS—ALL PLAYS (See Plate 7.)
The high triangle above each of the Angel's eyes is important and differs for each play. Rudolf Steiner would often do the make-up personally for the actor or actress playing each Angel.

Each eyebrow should make a high angle above the eye and be drawn in blue. A brownish red (theatre make-up No. 9 is recommended) should go under the brow. White should go between the eyes and on each side of the bridge of the nose. The eyes should be drawn also in blue and *made as large as possible.*

CHARACTERS IN THE PARADISE PLAY

TREE-SINGER: young man
ANGEL: preferably acted by a woman
GOD
ADAM: young man
EVA: young woman
DEVIL: preferably acted by a man

PARADISE PLAY

The curtains open (see Director's notes 1 and 8), pp. 9 and 10. All positions and moves are indicated as seen from the Audience.

(The Tree-singer enters from the wing downstage right, looking around, as if he is looking for the way. He discovers the tree and then the Audience, showing his surprise. Excitedly, he calls the Company)

TREE-SINGER   Come
(God and Angel enter from the wing downstage right and Devil, Eva and Adam from the next wing upstage. They form a flattish curve behind Tree-singer, who stands centre front stage. From left to right: Devil, Eva, Adam, God and Angel)
    Players and singers, rejoice and be glad,
    I tell you great honour this day you have had,
    The whole worshipful town is gathered today
    To hear your singing and mark your play.
    So heartily, lads, each tune sing true,
    And show these good folk what you can do.
    Put on your best faces;
(All smile)
                                   let each word tell;
    And sound me your notes as clear as a bell.
    But first your greetings to one and all,
    Together assembled in this hall.
(Tree-singer takes his hat off and keeps it off, and the Company bow three times: centre, their left, their right)
    God bless the Father on his high throne,
(All bow to the centre)
    And God bless his only begotten Son,
(All bow to their left)
    God bless the Holy Spirit also

That he leads our souls the way we should go,
(All bow to their right)
And God bless both Father and Spirit and Son,
Most Holy Trinity, Three Persons in One.
(All bow three times: centre, their left, and their right. All bow to everyone and everything during the Tree-singer's speech)
Greet Adam and Eva
(All bow to them and they bow back)
                      and each bird and beast
In Paradise here, both greatest and least
(All bow to 'tall and 'small' beasts, in front and around them)
And greet me the firmament that God's hand
Did make at the end of the world for to stand.
(All greet with the right hand, making a large, sweeping gesture towards the heavens from stage left to right)
Our parish as well we may never forget,
So greet me the Council and all of their set,
(All bow to an agreed place)
(Now the Tree-singer looks as if he is searching for someone and finds him)
And the one above all who sits in the Chair,
Come greet him—God's will must have put him there.
(All bow to that person)

(Here, at Michael Hall School, Sussex, and in other institutions it is the tradition to improvise greetings relevant to the Audience, then)

And now, my good singers, strike up again,
And greet yonder tree with a lusty refrain:
Of the fruit of that tree man never should eat,
If so be he'd keep a right watch on his feet.
So greet me the tree that of all bears the crown,
(All bow to the tree)
And likewise the apples that from it hang down.
(All bow to the apples; the Tree-singer, rising up from bowing, sees Eva who, as he speaks, turns away in shame)

But O, that wretched Eva she ate of the fruit,
And with her that booby
(On the word 'booby' Adam opens the veil briefly, giving the Audience the 'hope' to see who it is)
                        called Adam to boot,
So God cast them out for the sin of their deed
Of which in our hearts we should ever take heed.
For the Devil alone
(Tree-singer makes a little expectant pause . . . The Devil hearing his name comes proudly forward, but on the word 'fail' returns, offended, to his place, turning his back to the cast)
                        Our greetings shall fail—
(To the Audience)
May God keep us from him.
(To the Company)
Let's all pull his tail.
(The whole Company goes towards the Devil ready to pull his tail. Devil turns around and frightens them. They go back to their places)
TREE-SINGER *(To the Company and also to the Audience)*
And now, my good singers, when Adam fell
How things were changed, you know it well;
So last greet our Master, the bravest of hearts,
Who—without many blows—licked us into our part
(Here it is the tradition to remember Rudolf Steiner, who first revived and produced the Plays)
Good friends, now you know what your old friend and true
Would have each dear singer and player to do.

(Tree-singer puts on his hat, goes in front of the Angel and leads the Company around the Audience, clockwise, and back to their places in a semicircle on the stage)

COMPANY *(Sing)*   O let me enter in this place
To sing with my heart's might,
And grant my mouth, O Lord, the grace
To sound thy praise aright.

In simple truth I rede
Thou art my God indeed;
Thou hast withouten aid
All things and creatures made.
Praise God for evermore!

But see, but see a tree stands here
Which precious fruit doth bear,
That God has made his firm decree
It shall not eaten be.
Yea, rind and flesh and stone
They shall leave well alone.
This tree is very life,
Therefore God will not have
That man shall eat thereof.

ANGEL *(Goes to centre front stage, in front of the Company, and speaks to the Audience)*
In right good faith I enter this place,
God give you good evening of his grace,
A right good evening, the best of cheer,
(Angel points to the Lord with his hand above the Audience)
The Lord of Heaven grant
(Showing people across the Audience)
                                        each man here.
Most reverent worship, both
(Angel shows one side of the Audience with one hand)
                                Master
(Angel shows the other side of the Audience with the other hand)
                                        and Dame
Our service.
(Angel bows. Then showing the 'maidens' across the Audience)
            To you, pretty maidens, the same.
(Angel bows)
We shall but trouble you, by your leave,
(Angel shows Adam and Eva)
While here of Adam and of Eve
Their woeful sin we shall you show,

From Paradise they needs must go—
(Angel holds two fingers before mouth)
    So, silence, gentles all we pray,
(With 'warmth' to the Audience)
    And grant your hearts to hear our play.

(Angel and Company bow to the Audience centre, their left, and their right. Angel returns to his place. Tree-singer leads the Company clockwise through the Audience with the next song. During the end of the song he leads the Company on the stage, this time passing behind the tree where Eva and Devil stay hidden. They go to their places 'peeling off' as the Company go round: God goes in front of his throne, where he stands, Angel stands on the left of God's throne, Adam goes to the front right, and Tree-singer goes in front of the podium on the right. At the end of the song **simultaneously***, Adam kneels and Tree-singer sits down)*

COMPANY *(Sing)*
    How fresh the morning doth appear,
    Before the sunrise we are here,
    To God on his throne,
    Our praise be shown.

    From Babylon we took our leave
    To sing you all this joyful stave,
    To God ...

    As God did in his Godhead brood
    He made the world and saw 'twas good,
    To God ...

    Yea, beastes all both small and great,
    And living man did he create,
    To God ...

    In the beginning God did found
    The earth, and made the welkin round,
    To God ...

He made the firmament also,
And two great lights therein to show,
To God ...

The one is day the other night,
For God hath made them both aright,
To God ...

He Adam made by his great skill
And set in Paradise to dwell,
To God ...

(God goes behind Adam, raises his hands high up and takes them down to make a large A. Then he steps aside on Adam's right side and blows with his left hand near his mouth, as if directing the breath. Lifting his arms, Adam throws the veil behind him. The Devil, who had gone quietly to hide behind the throne during the creation, runs quickly forwards and collects the veil; he then runs back, passing behind the throne, all the way to hide behind the tree)

GOD   Adam, the living breath essay
  I give thee with this light of day,
  And reason
  (Adam points to his forehead with two fingers of his right hand on the word 'reason')
        that thou know thy God
  Hath made thee living from the sod.
  But time it is thy life
(Adam makes a little 'L' eurythmy gesture in front of his chest on the word 'life')
        began,
  Stand on thy feet and be a man.
(Adam stands up, firmly planting his feet down, slightly apart)
  Say, Adam, how does the world doth strike thee?
  All fresh and shining—doth it like thee?
(Showing the garden around them)
  The earth with all its brave adorning

The sunshine of this first bright morning,
The firmament majestical,
What, Adam, art thou pleased withal?
Speak, man, I yearn to hear thy mind.

ADAM *(Looking in front of him, not at God)*
O Father, very good, I find
What in thy Godhead thou hast made,
My strength is in thy wisdom stayed,
My good to do thy holy will,
For thou hast made and keepest me still,
In me thine image is revealed.

(They move forwards in an anticlockwise curve, looking at what God mentions, Adam still in front and both with appropriate gestures)

GOD   Take thou the creatures of the field,
Adam, to thee they are assigned
To do thee service in their kind.
The earth with hills and mountains steep
I give thee, fishes of the deep
And birds of air, that by this hand
I made, I give to thy command.
Share thou with me my domination.
And be the lord
(Adam puts his right fist on his chest on the word 'lord')
         of all creation.
On thee a garden I bestow,
Master of all the trees that grow,
Whose branches with ripe fruit are bent
Which thou may'st eat to thy content.
One sole command (the rest is free)
I give thee now. Look on this tree
(By then they have arrived at stage right. God shows the tree with his right hand in a large gesture, and Adam looks at the tree)
Of good and evil, that doth stand

Hard in the midst of this fair land,
For that of trees it is most sweet,
Of this alone thou shalt not eat,
(Adam makes a 'NO' gesture with his hand)
But shouldst thou shameless prove and proud
And eat of this tree disallowed,
Then shalt thou perish in a breath
And die an everlasting death.
(Adam hangs his head in grief)
Whereby thou knowest thy God am I,
(Adam gradually lifts up his head)
Who make to live and make to die;
Yea, life and death as I ordain
I give and I can take again.

(Tree-singer stands up; Eva and Devil join the Company during the beginning of the song and Tree-singer leads the Company, with the song, in the same order, clockwise, through the Audience and back on the stage to the same places)

COMPANY *(Sing)*   Adam, thy Creator know,
Who did all things on thee bestow,
To God on his throne
Our praise be shown.

He gave the goodly fruits of earth
That thou might'st live withouten dearth,
To God, etc....

One tree he set aside of all,
That into harm thou might'st not fall,
To God, etc....

Knowledge it is of evil and good;
God spake it: write it in thy blood.
To God, etc....

God did cause a slumber deep
To fall on Adam and he did sleep,
To God, etc....

He took a rib from Adam's side,
And made a woman to be his bride.
To God, etc....

(Tree-singer sits down and simultaneously Adam kneels on one knee, his head bent on his hand, his elbow resting on the other knee, and falls asleep. God goes behind Adam, pulls out the rib with his right hand, holds it up and speaks)

GOD   I took a rib from Adam's side
(God goes clockwise behind the tree holding the rib up. He leaves the rib behind the tree and takes Eva by her left hand. He comes forward centre stage and presents Eva to the Audience)
And made a woman to be his bride;
(God drops Eva's hand—she is looking at the garden—and calls Adam, still asleep)
Adam,
(Adam does not wake up, so God gives him a slap on the back to wake him up! Eva looks on)
       awake and stand upright
(Adam rises)
Behold thy equal come to light.
Formed she is from out thy bone,
(Surprised, Adam looks at and feels with his left hand his bottom left rib)
Wherefore
(God brings the hands of Adam and Eva together)
       cleave thou to her alone.
(Adam and Eva bow their heads to receive the blessing; God raises his arms and hands above the heads of Adam and Eva)
My angel shall protect your ways,
My blessings be on all your days,
Be fruitful, multiply, fill the earth,
Ye shall have plenty withouten dearth,
(God makes a gesture of 'warning' with his right hand and Adam and Eva separate)
Be but obedient to my word.

ADAM Yea, that will I right well, O Lord,
And here receive what thou dost give,
All creatures and myself to live.
*(God returns to his throne in a clockwise direction, and sits down. Adam and Eva do **not** move until God is seated. Then they look at each other with curiosity, touch each other's arms . . . and then, overwhelmed with joy, Adam speaks)*
Look, Eva, in what happy wise
We here may live in Paradise;
God hath for us this garden set,
To dwell there without toil or sweat;
One sole command we must obey,
The Lord hath laid on us this day.
(They go round to visit the garden, Eva more curious and quicker, in the same curve, forward, anticlockwise, miming what they see)
But listen how the sweet birds sing,
And see the beastes leap and spring!
What goodly trees the Lord hath made,
With leafy boughs to give us shade,
And fruit that we may freely share—
Only one tree we must forbear,
(Showing the tree)
Midmost it stands, it is the best,
(Eva hurries towards the tree but Adam catches her and brings her back)
But of its fruit we must not taste;
For should we shameless prove and proud
And eat the tree he disallowed,
Then shall we perish in a breath
And die an everlasting death.
Whereby we know he is our God
Who made us living from the sod,
Yea, life and death, as he ordain,
He gives and he can take again.

(God and Tree-singer stand up simultaneously and Adam, Eva,

Devil join them to go around the Audience clockwise whilst they sing and return to their places on the stage)

COMPANY *(Sing)*
   Now are they filled with joy and bliss,
   All things are framed to their service,
   To God on his throne
   Our praise be shown.

   Of which the devil straight is ware
   And secretly he creepeth there,
   To God ...

   Yea, in a serpent's guise
   Dwelt there in Paradise.
   To God ...

(God and Tree-singer sit down simultaneously and Eva and Adam look at the garden on stage right. Lights darken slightly and are redder. Devil comes from behind the tree centre stage and goes to the front of the stage)

DEVIL *(Speaks to the Audience)*
   Here creep I into Paradise,
   Gliding in a serpent's guise,
   God hath created a woman and man
   And finished them off all spick and span
   And set them in his house and hall,
   But I'll soon see them over the wall.
   Therefore to Paradise I came up,
   And put it in their mind to sup.
   Now wherefore may they to their mind
   Eat of fruit of every kind,
   But this one tree, which is most sweet,
   Of this alone they may not eat?
(Speaks to Adam who has come forward stage right. Adam looks as if he is hearing the Devil around him and looks straight ahead; Eva has gone a little further upstage right, as if looking at the garden—but not too near the Angel!)

Adam, this fruit if thou wilt take,
Thou mayest be thy Lordes make;
(Adam refuses and moves away from the Devil, but the Devil insists by pulling his robe. Adam slaps his hand and marches across to front stage left. Devil spits after him and turns to Eva who has come forward, still looking at the garden. When she hears the Devil she stands still. During his speech the Devil gradually leads her towards the tree; Eva seems mesmerized by the tree and moves towards it until she is at its foot)
Eva, this apple take, as right
Thine own heart gives thee appetite,
And give to Adam that he bite.
(Lights come up slightly; God and Tree-singer stand simultaneously. Everyone stops acting and sings)

COMPANY *(Sing)*   An apple from the bow he brake,
Gave to Eva and she ate.
To God on his throne
Our praise we make known.

(God and Tree-singer sit down simultaneously. Lights darken slightly. The Devil observes with interest the scene that follows. Eva goes towards Adam and stands now in front of the tree)

EVA   Adam, sith man and wife we be,
I pray thee, look on yonder tree,
(She shows the tree with her left hand)
Whereon such lovely fruit abound,
The like of them I never found.
(The Devil during her speech has prepared an apple by polishing it. He now puts it in her left hand. Eva is filled with wonder when she sees the apple)
EVA *(Begging Adam)*   Now to taste it give me leave;
(Adam indicates 'No' with his hand and moves away towards the front stage left. Eva comes as forward as possible front stage, looking at the apple, as if mesmerized. Then she looks up at the

Audience, pauses and takes a bite. Simultaneously Devil gives a little jump for joy! Lights get a little redder)
EVA *(To the Audience)*　　As I am an honest Eve,
　It is heart's good to eat thereof.
(Eva calls Adam, who turns towards her and seems horrified)
　Adam, and thou do me love,
　Take and bite it in all haste,
　It hath so wonderful a taste.
(As Adam hesitates Eva takes his hand and puts the apple into it)

ADAM　　If of this apple I do eat
　It is that thou doth me entreat;
　I eat not of my will alone.
(Adam bites in the apple, and throws it to the ground towards the 'wing' on his right. Then he puts his hand to his throat and gives a cry; simultaneously the Devil jumps for joy and runs to hide behind the tree as lights go darker)
　Ah! How my soul is overthrown!

(Lights come up slightly; God and the Tree-singer stand up simultaneously. Everyone stops acting and sings)

COMPANY *(Sing)*　　Adam on that apple fed,
　And his eyes were opened,
　To God on his throne
　Our praise we make known.

　And when he ate it, in that hour
　All the world was wounded sore
　To God on his throne
　Our praise we make known.

(God and Tree-singer sit down simultaneously. Adam and Eva come together and look desperate and ashamed. Lights darken even more and become redder. Devil comes from behind the tree centre stage and goes to the front)

DEVIL *(Speaks to the Audience)*
　I am the devil of wedded folk,

Well known to
(Shows people in the Audience)
all who bear that yolk,
What sense they have they get from me,
Which is not more than it needs to be.
(Moves behind Adam and makes the gesture of hanging him)
The man shall hang himself for his trouble,
(Crouches next to Eva, looking up at her smirking and mocking, showing 'drowning' at her feet. Goes behind Adam and Eva and pretends to put a crown on their heads)
The woman shall drown herself bubble, bubble,
A Martyr's crown will fit them well,
And they'll get their grave with me in Hell.
(Speaking to the Audience)
Adam and Eve I have so cheated
And by my cunning so entreated
That God's command they have set aside,
And eaten what the Lord denied
(Spits at the feet of Adam and Eva)
Good end to vermin such as they,
(Twirls and jumps)
O what a marvellous trick to play!—
(Goes to the very front of the stage and speaks to the Audience)
I don't for nothing give apples away.
(Goes back slightly, pointing at Adam and Eva)
If Adam and Eve had eaten plum-cake
They wouldn't have caught such a belly-ache.
(Laughing, Devil goes back upstage to hide behind the tree; lights go up slightly)

ADAM *(Desperate)*   Ah, how my soul is overthrown!
O wife, I have great evil done,
That I have hearkened unto thee.
(God stands and goes to take his position centre upstage, and the lights on him grow brighter)
A naked sword aloft I see,
(Adam crosses his arms in front of him, and Eva imitates him too)

And naked all and stark am I,
O wife, we have sinned grievously!

GOD *(Lights bright)*
Adam, where art thou? Come here to me.

(Adam takes a few steps towards the centre front stage and Eva, frightened, hides beside the tree, away from God)

ADAM   O Lord here am I.
Before thine eyes I am ashamed.

GOD   Why art thou ashamed?

ADAM   For that thy covenant I have slighted.

GOD *(Severe but not 'cross')*
Thinkest thou it shall go unrequited,
When one tree only I forbade thee?
Say, who did unto this persuade thee?

ADAM *(Takes a small step towards God)*
Ah, Lord I swear it on my life,
Eve, whom thou gavest me to wife,
She took the fruit and gave to me,
Would God that I had let it be.
She brake an apple from the bough,
And bit therein, and showed me how,
And brake in that same hour thy word,
E'en as thou camest hither, Lord.

GOD   Where is thy wife? Show her to me.

ADAM   Here, Lord, she stands beneath the tree.
(Adam Fetches Eva and pushes her gently forward towards the front of the stage)

GOD   Eva, say on. What hast thou done?

EVA   Ah Lord, the snake did so persuade
I took the fruit thou hadst forbade,
And gave to Adam of my store.
Ah Lord, we will not do it more!
(Adam and Eva go near each other on the next words)

GOD   Angel Gabriel, come hither to me.
(Angel moves towards God—see note p. 10. Devil brings the sword from behind the tree and puts it in God's extended right hand. He takes it below the handle, by the 'flame', and does not look at the Devil)
This naked sword I give to thee,
(God passes the sword to Angel. Angel takes the sword by the hilt and holds it in front of him)
That therewith Adam and Eva wise
Thou drive them out of Paradise,
And by my glory, power, honour,
They come within it never more.
(Tree-singer stands up. While singing the Company remain standing still and stop acting)

COMPANY *(Sing)*
There came an Angel with flaming sword,
And drove them forth before the Lord.
To God on his throne
Our praise we make known.

(Tree-singer and God sit down simultaneously. Adam and Eva are together again as before)

ANGEL *(Coming forward to front stage right, holding the sword in front of him)*
Lo, a command most sure have I
Received from God, the Lord Most High,
That Adam now and Eva wise
I drive them forth from Paradise.

(Makes a strong step, and swings the sword towards and above the heads of Adam and Eva. Simultaneously, they take a step together forward to stage left, Adam on Eva's right side, both going away from the Angel)
    From Paradise you needs must go,
    To till the soil with labour slow.
(Another step and swing. Adam and Eva too take another step, going away from the Angel)
    Adam! Thou in fear and dread
    With thy brow's sweat shalt win thy bread;
(Another step and swing. Adam and Eva also take a step)
    Eva, for thou this fruit has ta'en,
    Shalt bring forth children with great pain.

EVA *(Moving back towards the Angel, but speaking to the Audience)*
    Alas, poor womankind, that I
    Should bring them to this misery,
(With resolve and courage)
    But sith 'tis so, we must be bold
    Ourselves subject to God to hold,
    And keep in all things his decree.

ADAM   My dearest wife come here to me,
(Comes forward and in front of Eva towards centre stage)
    Not long, not long, Lord, I implore,
    But call us quickly home once more.

(The Angel takes another step and swing. Adam 'falls' back to his place. Eva and Adam take another step together again going away from the Angel)

ANGEL   Out of this place together go,
(Angel takes the sword back in a sweeping gesture and puts the point down on the floor in front of him)
    I shall recall you late and slow.

EVA *(Turns back)*   My God, forsake me not I pray!

ANGEL *(Stretching his right arm towards Eva)*
   Eva, cast thou thy doubts away,
(Showing Adam)
   Cleave to thy husband,
(Showing the Audience)
                     thy children tend
   So God forgive thee at the end.

(Angel returns to his place. God and Tree-singer stand up simultaneously. While singing the Company remain standing still and stop acting)

COMPANY *(Sings)*   Adam thus and Eva wise
   Are driven out of Paradise.
   To God on his throne
   Our praise we make known.

(God and Tree-singer sit down simultaneously. Lights dim and become very red. Adam and Eva come together very frightened)

DEVIL *(Comes from behind the tree centre stage carrying chains, which he throws on the floor front of stage)*
   I have beguiled this precious pair
   And out of Paradise lied them fair;
   But trust me for an eye to find them,
(Picks up the chains)
   And chains to snap and straitly bind them.
(Throws chains to the floor)
   Lord Ruler, I cry Murder, Haroo,
   On Adam and Eve, these culprits two,
   Who thy commandment, Sire, have slighted—
   I know it shall not go unrequited.
   They've fallen into the world of sin,
   Where trouble's always creeping in;
   And there I'm mostly to be found,
(Miming what he is saying, and running about, making more and more noise)

Looking about me and puffing around.
With a rant and a roar I arrive pell-mell—
(To the Audience)
It isn't exactly quiet in Hell.
(Blows towards Adam and Eva)
I'll blow the fires to a gentle heat,
(Adam and Eva come together even more)
And, Lord, how Adam and Eve shall sweat!
(God stands and walks to the centre upstage. The lights on him are brighter. Devil picks up the chains)
I'll bind them for thee with iron band,
(Puts the chains around Adam and Eva's shoulders)
And none shall snatch them out of my hands.

GOD *(Majestically, very stern but **not** 'angry')*
Get thee gone, Satan,
(Devil lets go of the chains. Adam takes the chains from Eva's shoulders and puts them on his own)
                thou hound of Hell,
Knowest thou not what a shameful word thy lips have let fall!
The dust of the earth shall be thy food
And on thy belly thou shalt crawl
Against the use of beastes all.
(Devil falls on the floor and remains immobile until the end of God's speech)
See now, this Adam such wealth has won
Like to a God he is become,
Knowledge he has of evil and good,
(Adam lifts his right hand)
He can lift up his hand on high,
Whereby he liveth eternally.

(Devil and Tree-singer stand up simultaneously. The Company form and Tree-singer leads them clockwise through the Audience and back onto the stage, Devil following God, then Eva and Adam. They all form a semicircle)

COMPANY *(Sing)*   O Holy Trinity,
O Godlike Sovereignty,
Who death and the fiend and Hell,
By your great might did quell,
And unto us do give
Eternal life to live,
We praise you evermore.
He who can read our mind
Grant us his realm to find.

(Angel gives the sword to Tree-singer, who takes his hat off, then Angel comes to the front centre stage)

ANGEL
Most reverend Worships, both Master and Dame,
Our service.
(Angel bows. Then showing the 'maidens' across the Audience)
          To you pretty maidens, the same,
(Angel bows)
I come but to say, now all is ended
We trust that in naught we have offended.
We have but shown Almighty God
He hath made all, and from the sod
Adam in stark and naked state
In his own image did create;
(Angel points to the Devil)
But the snake so tempted Adam and Eve
That God's commandment they did leave
On fruit which he forbad to feed
(Angel makes a downward gesture during his speech)
Whereby they fell in fear and need,
An everlasting death to end,
(Angel makes a large open gesture)
Till of his mercy God did send
His Son, who is his Son alone,
For sin of man to make atone.
(In a lighter tone!)

So think no evil, nor chide our play,
But if in ought we have gone astray
And shown your Worships what was not fit,
Blame not our will
(Lifting up and letting down his arms as in a 'sorry' gesture)
                        but our lack of wit.
Think it but well, so all's made right—
And we wish you from God Almighty, Good Night.

(The Angel and the Company bow: centre, their left, their right. Angel goes back to his place and takes the sword back, point up. Tree-singer puts his hat on and leads the Company through the Audience and out of the back of the Auditorium)

COMPANY *(Sing repeat of song)*   O Holy Trinity,
   O Godlike sovereignty ...

THE END

CHARACTERS IN THE SHEPHERDS PLAY

ANGEL: preferably acted by a woman
MARY: young woman
JOSEPH: older man
STAR-SINGER: young man
GALLUS: young man
HUCKLE: the youngest of the three shepherds
MUCKLE: older man
CRISPIN: very old man
INNKEEPERS: either men or women

SHEPHERDS PLAY

The curtains open. (See Director's notes 1 and 8), pp. 9 and 10. All positions and moves are indicated as seen from the Audience.

(The Company enter, singing, from the back of the Audience in the following order: Angel, Mary, Joseph, Star-singer—who opens the star-scissors, with the star above Mary—Gallus, Huckle, Muckle, Crispin, Rufinus, Servilus, Titus.
  Star-singer, Shepherds, Innkeepers go in front of the stage. Angel, Mary and Joseph go on the stage and stand in a triangle with Angel in front—the apex. Mary is behind to his left, and Joseph behind to his right)

COMPANY *(Sing)*   Bless, O Lord, the way we tread,
  Bless our coming and our going;
  Bless likewise our daily bread,
  Bless our leaving and our doing,
  Bless our death with thy death's leaven
  That to us thy life be given.
(Company in front of the stage mingle)

STAR-SINGER
  Come, gather round me my merry choir,
(Shepherds and Innkeepers gather very near him)
  Like chestnuts roasting round the fire.
  Spread yourselves, Masters.
(They go to their places. From right to left: Gallus, Huckle, Muckle, Crispin, Rufinus, Servilus, Titus)
                              Fill your lungs—
  But ere you sing your lusty songs,
  In God's name greet me one and all,
  And on the Trinity first we call.
(Tree-singer, Shepherds and Innkeepers remove their hats)

God bless God himself on his heavenly throne
(The whole Company, including Mary, Joseph and Angel, bows to the centre)
God bless the Son
(All bow to their left)
God bless the Holy Ghost
(All bow to their right)
God bless them as Three; and God bless them as One.
(They bow to the centre, their left, their right. Star-singer indicates Mary and Joseph, and everyone turns towards them)
God bless good man Joseph and Mary his spouse,
(Angel and Company bow to Mary and Joseph who bow back)
And God bless the stable that stood them for house.
(They turn and all bow to the crib, including the Angel, Mary and Joseph, and look at, bow to or greet everyone and everything mentioned)
And God bless the Child that was born in the stable.
(Deep bow to the Child)
And the ox and the ass that stood by his cradle.
(Two small bows or waving of hands)
God bless sun and moon and the stars of the night
(All greet making a larger sweeping gesture with left hand, from their right to left, towards the heavens)
And God bless the darkness that makes them so bright
(All bow)
And the grass, and the dew on the grass,
(All look at the grass, extend their hand towards it)
and the weather
God bless it, that wets you and us, Sirs, together.
(All bow with good humour)
God bless the King (Queen) with his (her) sceptre and crown
(All bow)
And God bless the Council and the Mayor of this town.
(All bow)

(Here, at Michael Hall School, Sussex, and in other institutions it

is the tradition to improvise greetings relevant to the local Audience)

And now, my fine singers, this way turn your hand
And greet me the Star, and the staff where it stands,
*(The Company turn to the Angel staff and they all bow, including Mary, Joseph **and** Angel)*
And greet the Star-scissors, though nothing they cut,
God bless them open—
(All bow)
                        and God bless them shut.
(All bow)
And the bolts and the bars, so stout and so strong,
God bless them that carry the brave Star along.
(All come near to greet and to touch the 'bars', and finally, as a result, the Star-singer pokes Rufinus in his fat stomach or pinches his fingers)
And our Master, who learned every player his part,
Until, with God's help, we had got them by heart,
(All bow. Here it is a tradition to remember Rudolf Steiner who first revived and produced the Plays)
And lastly God bless all good folk in this hall.
And God bless the blessing we've spoken for all.
(All bow to centre, their left and their right. The Shepherds and Innkeepers put their hats on. Star-singer goes in front of Gallus and leads the Company to join the Angel, Mary and Joseph on the stage as they sing. The Angel leads the Company anticlockwise along the benches, then along the back of the stage, behind the tree and out through the upstage left wing. Mary stays on centre front stage, with her arms crossed over her heart—reverence in eurythmy)

COMPANY *(Sing)*   When God the Almighty Lord
Would keep his promised word,
All for that blessed end
His Angel he did send,
And Gabriel his name.

Unto Nazareth he came
And Mary on that day
Saluted with AVE,
Who was unto her own
Betrothed man unknown.

(Angel enters, without his/her staff, from the downstage left wing, and goes to Mary's right side. Angel greets Mary with a deep bow, almost kneeling and arms down. Mary shows surprise and fright with a small gesture, and then Mary puts her hands together as in a gesture of prayer. Angel stays a step behind Mary)

ANGEL Hail, thou gracious one,
God the Lord is with thee,
Blessed art thou among women.
Behold thou shalt conceive,
And bring forth a Son,
And shalt call his name Jesus—
(Angel kneels, holding left arm raised and right arm down making an 'i'—EE in eurythmy. Mary also makes a small 'i' gesture: left hand straight and up connected to right hand straight and down, palms inwards. Then the Angel rises up and opens his/her arms in a gesture showing the Audience, and Mary folds her arms back to the 'reverence' position)
And he shall be a Lord over his folk for ever.

MARY How shall this be,
Seeing I know not a man?

ANGEL *(Speaking to the Audience)*
Behold, I am the Angel Gabriel
(Speaking to Mary)
That proclaim it unto thee.
(Angel's left hand high above Mary, in a blessing gesture)
The Holy Ghost shall come upon thee.
And the power of the Highest shall overshadow thee,
(Angel's left hand down, showing Mary)

Therefore also that Holy Thing which shall be born of thee
(Angel opens his/her arms and looks high above the Audience)
Shall be called the Son of God.
(Angel's left hand above Mary's right hand, waist high, palms upwards, in a more intimate mood; Mary turns slightly towards the Angel)
And behold thy cousin Elizabeth
She hath also conceived a son in her old age.
And this is now the sixth month with her
Whose reproach it was to be called barren.
(Angel makes a large gesture, steps back and looks up over the Audience)
For with God all things are possible.

MARY   Lo, I am the Lord's handmaid.
May it come to pass with me as thou hast said.
(Mary folds her arms in the 'reverence' gesture)

(Angel bows low again and goes offstage—not backwards—to fetch his staff and the Company, then leads the Company across the stage from downstage left. Mary takes her place as the Angel goes by. As they sing the Angel leads the Company through the Audience clockwise. At the end of the song the Angel returns to front stage centre and Mary leads the rest of the Company down in front of the stage)

COMPANY *(Sing)*   So while Mary is with child
In Augustus' day
See the prophecy fulfilled
No man can gainsay.
Caesar sendeth forth decree
All the folk shall taxed be
In their number truly,
Now upon the appointed morn
To the place where they were born
All betake them duly.
(Men take their hats off)

ANGEL   In right good faith I enter this place,
God give you good evening of his grace,
A right good evening, the best of cheer,
(Angel shows the Lord with his/her left hand high above the Audience)
The Lord of Heaven grant
(Angel shows people across the Audience)
                                  each man here.
Most reverent Worship
(Angel shows one side of the Audience)
                                both Master
(Angel shows the other side of the Audience)
                                    and Dame
Our service
(Angel bows. Then showing the 'maidens' across the Audience)
To you, pretty maidens the same
(Angel bows)
  Pray of your courtesy this day
For one brief hour to mark our play
We bring you here no heathen tale,
Nor things men gossip o'er their ale,
Which for your Worships were all unfit,
(Angel makes a 'teaching' gesture)
  But all is ta'en from Holy Writ;
Namely of Christ and Christes birth,
Who for our help was man on earth.
(Angel holds two fingers before mouth)
  So, silence, good men all we pray
(With warmth)
  And grant your hearts to hear our play.

(Angel taps the staff and the whole Company makes three bows: centre, left and right. Angel goes across the stage from centre to right and goes in front of Mary. Angel leads the singing Company through the Audience, clockwise, and takes everyone back onto the stage, passing behind the tree, to their places in front of the benches. As the Company go round, the Innkeepers 'peel' off

to their different entrances: Servilus to the left wing, Titus to the back centre of the stage and Rufinus to the right wing. Mary and Joseph go to the centre front stage, slightly to the left.
   Angel gives the sign with his/her staff, tapping it on the ground. The Company and Angel sit down simultaneously and remain immobile, and the Innkeepers, at the same time, exit into their 'inn'—the wings)

COMPANY *(Sing)*   Great Caesar from his royal throne
  Hath spoken that his will be done.
  Take tribute, ride from town and shire,
  Bring gold and goods to his desire.

  Joseph is risen and gone down
  With Mary to the taxing town,
  Who straightway as the journey's done
  In Bethlehem bringeth forth her son.

JOSEPH   Caesar Augustus has made decree
  All the world shall taxed be,
  On every house the tribute laid
  Straight and strictly must be paid,
  Or all its goods shall forfeit be.
  Ah God, what will become of me?
  What shall I do? Where shall I turn?
  My daily bread I scarce can earn.
  My shaky hand and dimming eye
  No more avail my craft to ply,
  And all I have, my little store,
  Scarce keeps the wolf from out the door.
  Yet needs I must the tribute pay
  And Caesar's dread decree obey.

MARY   Ah, Joseph, be not in such fear,
  I know a good man dwelling near
  Will give us help and timely rede
  And lend us money in our need.

JOSEPH   And pray where will you find the friend
That has so great a sum to lend?
Gold groweth not on every tree—
Nay, wife, talk not of such to me.

MARY   Husband, one thing is left us still
Whereby to do Augustus' will.
Come, let us drive our ox to town,
(Mary indicates the ox in the left wing)
And when to Bethlehem we come down,
Sell him at market the best we may,
And so get the money the tax to pay.

JOSEPH   Without our ox how shall we stead?
Where shall we look for daily bread?
As well might Caesar take life and blood
As the beast that gains our livelihood.
Yet all you say and more must we do.
(Speaking to himself)
I doubt the ox will pay for two.
(Joseph pretends to fetch the ass and to give it to Mary)
Take you the ass—on him you may ride,
And I with the ox will journey beside.
(He looks as if he is pushing the ox with his staff and they start walking, in step. But Mary, after a few steps, stops Joseph and speaks anxiously)

MARY   But in the crowded city's wall
Where shall our cattle find a stall?

JOSEPH   I know an innkeeper, by name
Rufinus, and my friend—the same
Shall ease us well with bite and sup
And put our weary cattle up.

MARY   But how if others come before
And house be full, and they shut the door?

For many the folk, both young and old,
That ride to the taxing when all must be told.

JOSEPH   Fear not; the town lies here before
Come, let us prick our beasts the more,
Lest doors be barred and folk abed,
And on cold stone we rest our heads.

(They continue the journey going anticlockwise on the stage and passing behind the tree. When they reappear from behind the tree, Joseph sees the town 'across stage' and goes faster)

MARY *(Calls him back)*   Ah Joseph be not in such a haste
Too heavy am I to go so fast.
The way with ice is coated o'er
To slip and fall I tremble sore,
My limbs with cold are numb and dead,
And of some evil I have great dread.

JOSEPH *(Going back to Mary and putting his arms around her shoulders)*
   This evening you shall warm them through
   By good inn fire, I promise you.
   For see, before the house I stand,
   And shall my friend's good help command.
(They go to Rufinus' door, stage right. Joseph knocks with his staff on the floor, Rufinus comes out)
   Rufinus, my friend, now welcome us right—
   Hast thou not lodging for us this night?
   Needs not to say, what thou well canst see,
   Full weary we come from a far journey.
   Hard in our face the North did blow,
   And battered us sore with ice and snow.

RUFINUS *(Phlegmatic)*
   My friend you must apply next door,
   My house is packed from roof to floor.

You are not the first—this very day
I've turned them by the score away.
(Joseph makes a begging gesture)
I am Master of this Hostelry
And order my house in my degree.
(Rufinus exits)

JOSEPH   Alas, this was my only friend,
Except the Lord some other send—
Come, let us try our luck elsewhere,
A good heart never knows despair.
(Showing the 'inn' on the other side of the stage)
The neighbouring host we'll kindly greet,
And call for lodging, drink and meat.
(Joseph and Mary go to Servilus' door and Joseph knocks with his staff on the floor. The Audience hears Servilus come from a long way with stamping feet. Servilus appears)
God bless you, friend, we would enquire
Have you a room that we could hire?

SERVILUS *(Choleric)*
What's this? Bah! Beggars, on my life,
What care I, fellow, for you and your wife?
(Gesture to show money)
I take in folk with money in purse,
(Kick towards Joseph)
And keep for tramps a kick and a curse.
(Joseph makes a begging gesture)
Pack up, the pair of you. Off from my door.
Don't trouble us here with your din any more!
(Servilus exits angrily. During the next speech Titus enters from the centre backstage with his lantern alight enquiring about the noise)

MARY   Dear God, in mercy hear our call
Let not such scorn on poor folk fall.
Need must we die of frost and fear
For certain no other lodging is near.

TITUS *(Who has arrived at the place where Mary and Joseph stand)*
    What, lass? So full of tears and cries?
    Come: mean you to weep out your eyes?
    My house is full and it grieves me sore
    That I cannot open to you my door.
    But if you would lie in the stable here
    You are welcome and more to such poor cheer.

MARY   Ah, good mine host, we stand not in mind
    This night to lie soft on a goose feather bed.
    We ask but a wall to ward the wind
    And a roof to keep the snow from our head.

TITUS   Come, enter then—till it befall
    My house have room—
(He shows the crib)
                      within this stall.
(Mary sits on the stool, Joseph stands next to her, and Titus gives him the lantern. Titus returns and exits through his door. Joseph puts the lantern down at the foot of the crib)

JOSEPH *(Sings)*   O maiden, here is shelter o'er thee,
    Here is a little cradle for thee,
    Where we with God shall sleep
    Who made and shall us keep.

MARY *(Sings)*   Ah, Joseph mine,
    Thou must my comfort be alone:
    The time draws near that I must bear
    With pain and many a grievous moan
    My little child, my Jesukin.

JOSEPH   Tomorrow with the break of day
    I must be stirring and away,
    In Cana market my ox to set,
    And see what offers I shall get;

Then with the money back to town
Post-haste, and pay the tribute down.

MARY A single ox will sell so dear,
Think you, to pay the tribute clear?

JOSEPH Nay, never doubt when I come back
No single farthing shall we lack.

*(The Angel rises and walks **very slowly** in front of the benches, along the back of the stage, behind the tree during Mary and Joseph's dialogue. At the end of the dialogue the Angel is standing behind the tree)*

MARY Ah, Joseph, now the hour is come
To loose the burden of my womb,
Fulfilled is Gabriel's word aright
And I must bear my child this night.
Then pray you again mine host to rouse
And beg he take us in his house.

JOSEPH Alas, my mind misgives me sore
We'll fare no better than before.
Yet will I knock and tirl the pin,
And beg he give us room within.

(Joseph picks up his lantern and goes towards Titus' door and stops there, his back to the public. Mary kneels in front of her stool. Joseph and the Company bow their heads down. The Angel appears behind Mary and lifts his left hand in a blessing gesture above Mary's head, and holds the star on the staff high above Mary. Mary opens her arms, lifting them to make an 'O', then brings them down together as if she were holding a baby. As Mary brings her arms down, the Angel lowers the star following Mary's arm movement. Lights go brighter and stay bright. Angel exits through the wing nearer to where he/she was standing. The

Company lift their heads. Joseph comes back, sees the Child and in great excitement goes back to Titus' door and knocks the floor with his staff. Titus appears.)

JOSEPH   Sir Titus, hearken to our plight,
  A child is born to us this night,
  And we all frozen in yon shed—
  Open, and give us board and bed.

TITUS   Gladly, Old Sir, I would you please,
  You and your wench and do you ease;
  But here lie four and twenty head
  Packed like peas-in-pod abed,
  And folk asprawl on bench and floor—
  Knock, friend, at some neighbour door
(Joseph makes a begging gesture, Titus shakes his head)
  I'm Master of this Hostelry.
  And order my house in my degree.
(Titus exits)

JOSEPH *(Comes back to Mary)*
  Mary, our prayers are all denied
  In stable still we must abide,
  But see, for cold our babe doth cry,
  Lay we him in this manger nigh,
  Where ox and ass, on either hand,
  To warm him with their breath do stand.

MARY *(Sings)*   Ah, Joseph mine,
  Why is this world so faithless grown
  To spurn us out of house and hall
  And leave us in a cattle stall?
  Ah, Joseph mine, Ah, Joseph mine,
  Reach down a sheaf of hay to spread,
  And make our child a bowry bed.
(Joseph helps with the hay to prepare the crib)

JOSEPH *(Sings)*   Dear heart, my love and all my joy,
Bring hither now thy little boy.
(Joseph helps Mary put the child in the crib; Mary sits down on her stool)

MARY *(Sings, rocking the crib)*   Ah, Joseph mine,
Help me rock our Little Boy,
God thereof shall give thee joy,
Ah, Joseph mine, Ah, Joseph mine.

JOSEPH *(Kneels and sings, while helping to rock the Child)*
O, thou dearest Mario,
Lullay I sing, lulli lullo,
I help thee rock thy Little Boy,
God thereof shall give me joy,
Mario, Mario!
(Joseph stands up)

MARY *(Sitting more upright, having stopped rocking the crib, sings)*
Ah, Joseph, Mary's angel sings,
Sings Gloria for these tidings;
The Love to earth is brought
For which we strove and wrought,
Our Little Child, Our Jesukin.

(Angel appears from the wing stage right and taps his/her staff. The Company stands and the Innkeepers come out of their door at the same time. Angel goes across the stage followed by the Star-singer, the Shepherds and the Innkeepers who take their places in the procession. As they go past the crib and the Child they bow and the Angel lowers the Star towards the crib. The direction of the procession is now reversed—anticlockwise—after the event of the Birth; Mary and Joseph stay on the stage. The Company return to the bench on stage, passing behind the tree, led by Angel, except for the Shepherds who leave the procession as it arrives on the stage. Crispin stays in the wing stage left. The other three Shepherds exit

backstage right. Muckle and Huckle quietly make their way, preferably outside, to the back of the Audience. The Angel exits from the right wing)

COMPANY *(Sing)*   A Child is born in Bethlehem,
This year, this year,
Wherefore exult Jerusalem,
This year we joy and sing.
We sing the Mother of Our Lord,
And Jesus her Sweet Boy,
And Christ we sing above all thing,
This year with mirth and joy,

Now lies he in a manger small,
This year, this year,
Who shall at last be Lord of all,
This year we joy and sing,
We sing the Mother of Our Lord,
And Jesus her Sweet Boy,
And Christ we sing above all thing
This year with mirth and joy.

(Angel taps his/her staff and the Company sit simultaneously. Angel exits through front right wing. Lights dim)

GALLUS *(Shouting from the wings upstage right)*   Ut Hoy!
(Enters and looks around enquiringly)
   What? Am I not last? I thought so to be,
   Yet nor Huckle nor Muckle before me I see.
   So freezing cold in face it blows
(Tries to feel his nose, very gently!)
   No longer can I feel my nose.
(During their speeches the Shepherds keep warm by slapping their arms around their bodies, rubbing their hands and stamping their feet)
   This day to Huckle, my good friend,
   I, Gallus, my two gloves did lend.

Then why away doth Huckle stay?
I look around ...

HUCKLE *(Shouting from the back of the Audience)*
Ut Hoy!

GALLUS   Lo, there at last
My brother Huckle comes right fast.
(He comes running up, jumps onto the stage and speaks to the Audience)
What? Am I not first? I thought so to be
But here brother Gallus before me I see.

GALLUS   Huckle, how fare our flocks on the wold?

HUCKLE   With thy sheep, Gallus, I was right cold.

GALLUS   Cold Huckle? Of that I am full sad.
But look on my two hands, my lad.
(Shows his two hands to Huckle)

HUCKLE
What? Hast thou but two? Thou liest by this head:
Take here a hundred of mine in their stead.
(He beats Gallus' hands quickly; Gallus' hands being freezing cold, this hurts him and he makes a show of it!)
But why away doth Muckle stay?
I look around ...
(They both search, turning around and at last see him in the Auditorium)

MUCKLE   Ut Hoy!
(Muckle being older does not come 'right fast' and Huckle mocks him gently)

HUCKLE   Lo, there at last
My brother Muckle comes 'right fast'.

MUCKLE   Ut Hoy!
What am I not first? I thought so to be,
But Gallus and Huckle before me I see.

(The Shepherds always stand in the same order. From left to right: Huckle, Muckle, Gallus. They act on the right-hand side of the stage, not in front of Mary and Joseph)

HUCKLE
Eh, Muckle hast been round the world? By this head,
Waiting for thee we were like to be dead.

MUCKLE   Aye, for my good wife would not let me out
Until I had stitched her shoes all about.
(Shows how to stitch a shoe, lifting his own foot with difficulty!)
But brothers, if this frost shall keep,
Must have a care of us and sheep.

GALLUS   Good Huckle, hast not heard men say
The Lord Cyrinus hath laid this day
A mighty tax on every head,
Which all must pay in fear and dread
That all their goods shall forfeit be?
Who now shall you find from terror free?

HUCKLE   Eh, Gallus what is't thou dost say?
A mighty tax that all must pay?
Is there no end to poor folk's need?
The last crumb taken of their bread?

MUCKLE   Great God, will taxes never bate?
Must trouble still on trouble wait?
T'is time the poor man's sweat and swink
Brought him at least his meat and drink.
A load of trouble I see in store,
And hunger stalking at every door.
(All three look gloomily into the far distance)

GALLUS   Ah, Muckle thou hast not to bewail,
  If thou talk of trouble, hear first my tale.
(Huckle shows that he has often heard this before and becomes impatient during Gallus' speech, intimating that he himself has stolen the sheep; he finally turns his back to Gallus)
  Sure never did shepherd such woes befall,
  By night or day I sleep not at all;
  I hold such watch and ward o'er my sheep,
  I scarce can tell when I last did sleep.
  Yestreen was I in field with my men,
  To count our sheep began we then,
  Full short was the tale we found by our tally—
(To Muckle)
  I shall you tell how they did miscarry

HUCKLE *(Turns back to speak to Gallus)*
  Say on; old gibberer.

GALLUS   One part—the wicked wolf has eaten them.
(Every time 'wolf' is mentioned the Shepherds look around them in fear!)

HUCKLE   Belike the butcher's dog had bitten them.
  So untoward this hap did befall—
  Must the wolf bear the blame for all?

GALLUS   What, must thy tongue be still a-jog?
  See, the wolf can bite you as hard as a dog.
(Gallus hits Huckle's crook with his crook)

HUCKLE   Nay, harder by this head.
(Huckle hits Gallus back, starting a fight. Muckle looks on concerned)

GALLUS
  What further wouldst say hereof, must thou keep.
  Time it is now to be watching thy sheep.

(Gallus gives a last push to Huckle and they both turn their back on each other, sulking. Muckle takes his bag of food from his shoulder and shows it to the other two, hoping to bring them back together. Whilst he speaks, Gallus and Huckle come back gradually interested by the food)

MUCKLE   Look you, my wife has put something up—
Turf cakes and pasties. What shall we sup?

HUCKLE   And is there no hunk of fat dripping, man?

MUCKLE   Whist!
Three pieces, and each as big as your fist!

(Gallus and Huckle help Muckle sit down. Muckle pulls out imaginary food and a bottle. Huckle takes off the gloves he had borrowed from Gallus and puts them on the ground. Muckle shares the food and they eat; then he passes the bottle around. Gallus drinks and gives the bottle back to Muckle, who passes it to Huckle. Huckle drinks greedily, and during this Gallus steals back the gloves with his crook, unseen by Huckle. When Huckle has finished drinking he realizes that Gallus has taken his gloves back. When Muckle wants to drink in his turn, he notices with good humour that the bottle is empty. When they have finished, Muckle collects the bottle and bag and starts speaking as he gradually gets up. Gallus and Huckle gradually get interested in what Muckle is saying; looking all the time at him, they kneel and finally stand. See Director's note 9, p. 12)

MUCKLE   Late have I heard it told in some fashion,
How God from eternity on men hath compassion,
And sendeth Messiah his word to fulfil,
To redeem and comfort men of good will,
The sickness of earth he shall amend,
And of all burdens shall make an end.

GALLUS *(Gallus and Huckle finally stand up)*
Ah, were that day already here,

That unto us Messiah appear,
For joy and bliss would we leap and spring,
And shout to God in thanksgiving.
(Bangs his crook and jumps for joy)
Ut Hoy!

HUCKLE and MUCKLE *(Banging their crooks and jumping for joy)*
Ut Hoy!

HUCKLE   O in what hour? And in what place,
Shall he be born that brings such grace?

MUCKLE   The hour we may not truly tell,
But of the place we know right well,
(Indicates Bethlehem to his left far in the Audience; they all look)
In Bethlehem born shall he be,
And of a choice maid certainly.
(On these words the Shepherds reflect dreamily, and become drowsy)

GALLUS   Now, brothers, be our will agreed,
I rede you rest is shepherd's need
So on the ground let each him lay
And sleep a little till it be day.

(They lie down swiftly, as if 'overcome'. Here one can play the Nocturno whilst the Angel comes on the stage from upstage right, looks for the Shepherds and walks among them. As the Nocturno ends the Angel is standing behind the Shepherds upstage. Lights go up slightly on the Angel's entrance, and when the Angel stops a spotlight shines on him)

ANGEL *(Sings)*   Gloria, Gloria in excelsis!
Joy, shepherds, Joy and good tidings
To you and all mankind I bring.
O shepherds, Christ wake you,

From slumber now shake you,
To Bethlehem betake you,
Shepherds each one.
(On the word 'run', occurring four times, the Shepherds move their legs in their sleep, as if running)
Run to the stable, to the manger, the cradle,
To the Young One, the Maid's Son, run shepherds, run.
Haste ye, O haste ye, here lies your way,
Take pipe, take tabor, and play, shepherds, play.
Run to Bethlehem, seek out the stall,
Greet the Youngling, one and all,
O you shepherds, be not cast down,
Hark to the news that I make known.

GALLUS *(Lifting his upper body slightly, speaks in his dream and the Angel shows that he is listening to the Shepherds)*
Eh, Huckle, who is this so late
That thus doth sing and jubilate?
Some ghost this night has lost his way,
And leads us in our dream astray.

HUCKLE *(As Gallus)*
I marvel greatly what this may be.
Somewhat under my hat did I see,
When lo, a great and shining light—
What should it be?—before my sight?

MUCKLE *(As Gallus)*
And in my ears a sound did ring.
Sure, none but Angels can so sing.

ANGEL *(Sings; Shepherds do **not** move during this song)*
From Heaven above to you I bring
A blessed word of good tiding.
Yea, News of joy and mirth this day
(To the Audience)
To all mankind I sing and say.

(Angel exits upstage right, spotlight dims and the lights come up as if it were dawn and gradually go brighter. Gallus wakes up, gets up and slips because the ground is frozen. Muckle also wakes up at the same time but being slower he is warned by Gallus)

GALLUS   Have a care, 'tis frozen over!

MUCKLE   Ay, blockhead, 'tis smooth as glass.
My beard is full of ice.
There's a patter of rain too!

(Gallus and Muckle see Huckle still asleep on the ground)

GALLUS *(Using his crook to try to lift Huckle, rolling him, but Huckle rolls back)*
Huckle, get up. The sky is cracking!

HUCKLE
Let it crack. It's old enough to have cracked before.
(He settles to go back to sleep)

GALLUS *(Again using his crook)*
Huckle get up. The little birds are singing!

HUCKLE
Let 'em sing. They've got small heads; they're soon awake.
(He settles to go back to sleep)

GALLUS *(Again using his crook)*
Huckle get up. The drivers are cracking their whips on the road!

HUCKLE   Let 'em crack 'em. They've far enough to go.
(He settles back to sleep)

(Both Gallus and Muckle use their crooks this time)

GALLUS   Come, man, thou must get up.

(Huckle gets up, slips and has a thunderous fall—Gallus making sure that Huckle is warned too late, his revenge at last on the gloves!)

GALLUS   Have a care, 'tis frozen over!

HUCKLE *(Carefully getting up, crossly)*
Frozen it is, by this head.
Couldst not open thy mouth to say so, before I laid open my brains?
(Furious, he brushes his coat and knees and as he does so he gradually remembers ... slowing down his brushing)
But Gallus, good Gallus, what hast thou dreamed,
That thou didst so mumble and rumble by me in thy sleep?
What hast thou dreamed then?

GALLUS   What have I dreamed?
That can I well say.

(They form a triangle facing inwards with Gallus at the apex, his back to the Audience; they bang their crooks together on the ground and jump around the crooks to face outwards. Gallus now faces the Audience for his singing)

GALLUS *(Sings)*   As by a stall I rode this night
Of ox and ass I saw a sight,
That from a manger fed,
O Child most rare, O Maiden fair,
That stood beside his bed.
And when I woke from slumber deep,
' 'fore God, I would a se'nnight sleep
For such a dream,' I said.

(They bang their crooks together, jump around them to face inwards and move on one place, going clockwise standing side by side)

HUCKLE
   But Muckle, good Muckle, what hast thou dreamed
   that thou dist so mumble and rumble by me in thy sleep?
   What has thou dreamed then?

MUCKLE   What have I dreamed?
   That can I well say.

(Same as before but this time Muckle is the apex of the triangle and faces the Audience when he turns around his crook)

MUCKLE *(Sings)*   All in the Holy Night so still
   A slumber deep upon me fell,
   And soon, as I lay sleeping,
   A sweetness like to honey stole
   Or fragrant roses on my soul—
   With joy my heart was leaping.

(They bang their crooks together, jump around them to face inwards and move on one place, going clockwise and standing side by side)

GALLUS
   But, Huckle, good Huckle, what hast thou dreamed
   that thou didst so mumble and rumble by me in thy sleep?
   What hast thou dreamed then?

HUCKLE   What have I dreamed?
   That can I well say.

(Same as before but this time Huckle is the apex of the triangle and faces the Audience when he turns around his crook)

HUCKLE *(Sings)*   I dreamed, and lo an Angel came
   And led us unto Bethlehem,
   In Judah's land so far.
   And there a wondrous thing befell,

Good news, good news on earth to tell,
In Heaven a shining star.

(They bang their crooks together, jump around and move on to their original places. Then they follow each other dancing and jumping but in step. Gallus leads then Huckle and Muckle. They can dance on the stage and through the Audience)

THREE SHEPHERDS *(Sing)*
Lusty, trusty shepherd boys,
That love to make a cheerful noise,
Heigh ho, foot it while you sing,
Evil fails and good doth spring.
David was a shepherd young,
David cheers both heart and tongue.

Lusty singing by our sheep,
When we have no mind to sleep;
Who to stop our mouths dare try,
Shouting praise to God most high?
Sing, lads, who shall say you nay?
David's self did sing and play.

After many a mighty stroke,
He shall raise his chosen folk,
Kings and potentates put down,
He shall wear at last the crown,
Every soul in David joys—
Are not shepherds lusty boys?
(They return to their places on the stage—from left to right: Huckle, Muckle and Gallus)

GALLUS   Have with you to Bethlehem, then, say I,
To see this sight beyond compare.
Yet what should we take to one so high,
What gift can we give when we come there?

HUCKLE *(Without hesitation)*
   A bottle of milk have I for this need
   That mother and child alike shall feed.

MUCKLE *(Pretending to hook a sheep with his crook—someone from the front row!)*
   A lamb, the best my flock can yield—
   Of which full worthy is such a child—
   On my two shoulders will I lift,
   And to that child will make a gift.

GALLUS   A bundle of wool with me will I take
   That his mother full soft his bed may make.

(They start their journey, going along the benches and then behind the tree, where they collect their gifts and put them in their coats. Muckle leaves the bag for their food behind and Gallus the gloves. All the while they walk in step, even when they collect their gifts. The lights dim to a very dark blue when the Shepherds reach the tree, so they can't be seen. When the Shepherds reappear from behind the tree they have lost their way and the rhythm of their stepping is broken; they go in all directions)

HUCKLE   So dark grows the night, no more can I say
   Whether or no we have lost the way.
   What say you fellow, go we right?

(The lights come up slightly on Mary and Joseph; Gallus sees it and calls the others)

GALLUS   Huckle, I see before me a light
   There let us go and ask them fair
   If God's Son haply be lodged there,
   Or beg they tell us, as best they know,
   Whither to find him we must go.
(They fall in step and go to the crib. Gallus knocks with his crook on the ground)

Hallo there. Open the door we pray.
Shepherds we are that would ask our way.

(Joseph picks up the lantern and moves towards the Shepherds; he holds the lantern high to see who is there)

JOSEPH My friend, let one among you speak
And freely say what here you seek.
With searching looks and eager mind
You come—what think you here to find?

HUCKLE It is God's Son we would find out
That lies in a stable hereabout.
For so to us it has been revealed,
And we seek him, leaving our flocks afield.

JOSEPH Come, enter then, if such your mind.
(Joseph indicates the Child; the Shepherds take a step forward and take off their hats. Lights come up warm and bright on 'here')
Here is the Child you look to find.

THREE SHEPHERDS *(Full of awe, looking at the Child, sing)*
Behold, my heart, what thing is here,
That in the crib so sweetly lies;
It is God's Son, his pretty one,
His Child, the youngling Jesus dear.

(Gallus kneels down, puts his crook and hat down on the floor)

GALLUS Greetings to thee, Child most rare,
That liest in a manger cold and bare.
No feather bed hast thou this day,
Thy pallet the spiky straw and hay.
Thou camest not with summer's rose
But with the winter's ice and snows,
And for thy lily thou must see
White fields of frost encompass thee.

Ah, youngling, pity it is to behold
Thy little cheeks so pinched with cold,
To see thy pretty golden eyes
Weep bitter tears, to hear thy cries.
(Pulls out the wool from his coat and presents it to the Child)
Look, little one, take this wool for thy bed,
Whereon thou softly mayst rest thy head.
(Puts the wool down at the foot of the crib, pulls out a bag of flour and presents it to the Child)
I bring thee, too, some meal to bake
That thy Mother may make thee therewith a cake,
(Puts the bag of flour on the floor at the foot of the crib)
And if again I come by the door
Thou shalt not fail of presents more.

(Huckle kneels down next to Gallus and puts his crook and hat on the floor. The three Shepherds will kneel so that Gallus is nearest to the crib and the others on a diagonal, with Muckle furthest away from the crib)

HUCKLE   Greetings to thee, Child most rare,
All stiff with cold thou liest there.
In Heaven thou hadst a mansion great,
Yet cold and naked is here thy state.
(Pulls the bottle of milk out of his coat and presents it to the Child)
Take thou this milk to stay thy weeping
Whereby I give me to thy keeping.
(Puts the bottle of milk on the floor at the foot of the crib)

(Muckle kneels down next to Huckle and puts his crook, his hat and, with great care, the lamb on the floor in front of him)

MUCKLE   Greetings to thee, Child most sweet,
Yea, little Jesus, God thee greet.
In cattle stall thou, King, dost rest,
Thy mother giveth thee her breast.
(Lifts the lamb to show to the Child)

I bring thee, King, this lambkin white
Wherein thou mayest much delight.
(Gets up a little to be able to put the lamb at the foot of the crib)

JOSEPH   Shepherds I thank you that you bring
Your gifts and worthy offering.

MARY *(Sings)*   Shepherds, I thank you that you bring
Your gifts and worthy offering.
God grant you sustenance, and keep
And bless from every harm your sheep.

(Gallus helps Mary rocking the crib. The other two Shepherds put their right hand on each other's shoulder and accompany the rocking by swaying slightly)

THREE SHEPHERDS *(Sing)*   Before the crib we kneel,
And him we rock and swing,
The Child that shall us heal,
And to him blessing bring,
Sweet Jesukin, sweet Jesukin.

(Shepherds rise slowly, picking up their crooks and hats; they bow low to the Child, then to Mary, then to Joseph. Mary and Joseph bow back. The Shepherds take a couple of steps, going upstage, led by Gallus who starts turning to his right; they stop and turn back to have a last look at the Child over their left shoulder. Then they put on their hats as they walk and go back to front stage right. They are pensive)

GALLUS   Eh, lads, how is't befallen thus
That he is born where none could guess?
In such poor place to see the day
Who doth the whole world rule and sway?

MUCKLE   On earth is he born in this poor fashion
So that on us he have compassion,

And make us rich in Heaven great
That like to angels shall be our state.
Yea, poorly is he born this day
That so from pride men turn them away,
And choose not riches and glorification,
But to live content in humble station.

HUCKLE   Now may we be of courage good
That he is born of kingly blood,
King David was a shepherd bred—
In holy writ so have I read—
That all alone with might and main
Goliath, that dread giant
(He bangs his crook loudly on he floor)
                                            hath slain!

GALLUS   But when we to our fellows tell
The sight that here to us befell,
They'll not believe what we report,
But will of us make mock and sport,
In such strange fashion is this bestead
It much may rack the wisest head.

MUCKLE   It were great peril that this be unknown;
Forthwith to the gentry it must be shown.
Tomorrow to Jerusalem will I repair
And tell it likewise to the mayor

(They dance and sing around the stage, in step, finishing at the front of the stage)

THREE SHEPHERDS *(Sing)*
Lusty, trusty shepherds boys,
That like to make a cheerful noise,
Heigh ho, foot it while you sing,
Evil fails and good doth spring.
David was a shepherd young,
David cheers both heart and tongue.

(Crispin enters from wing, front stage left. He is very old and very deaf and the shepherds have to speak loudly to him)

HUCKLE   See, Crispin, good Crispin cometh this way,
Who hath sought us without our yea or nay.
God give you good morrow, Crispin.

CRISPIN   I thank you in God's name, old friend.

GALLUS   How goes it with our sheep, Crispin?
(This can be repeated loudly twice: Crispin does not hear. But the third time, when Gallus speaks softly, then suddenly Crispin can hear!)

CRISPIN   Truly, the sheep in shippon do bide,
(He shows the size of sheep wrongly, indicating low for the big sheep and high for the little sheep)
Both the big and the little by their side;
But, brothers, what news have ye found out?
Is it true what makes such stir hereabout?

GALLUS   Truly in Bethlehem that child most high
Twixt ass and ox we saw him lie:
And wouldst thyself behold this sight,
Thou mayest rise with morning light
And with us to Bethlehem journey aright.

CRISPIN   Is it far to go?

GALLUS, HUCKLE, MUCKLE *(Together)*
Till thou comest there!

CRISPIN   Must think upon that child. Young Sir
Shall have a lappet of my fur.

FOUR SHEPHERDS *(Sing, walking around the stage)*
Thus the shepherds merrily

Their flocks and herds were keeping,
Meat they took, and down they lay
All together sleeping.
To them an Angel did appear,
And God shone about them clear,
That they were sore amazed.
The Angel spake, 'Fear you nothing,
Good news to all mankind I bring,
With joy your hearts be raised.'

(A small pause, then Angel enters front stage right and taps his/her staff. Company on the bench stand and all wait until Mary has picked up the Child and is ready to join the Company. Angel leads the Company, in their usual order, through the Audience anti-clockwise. They then come back on the stage where the Company form a large curve)

THE COMPANY *(Sing)*
Let all mankind rejoice this morn,
Both rich and poor be glad,
For unto us a Child is born,
And all things hath he made,
A Holy Child this same,
And Jesus Christ his name,
Who all for sinful man's misdeeds
To earth from Heaven came.

(Angel goes to the centre front stage, the Company behind him/her. The Company take off their hats)

ANGEL   Most reverends Worships,
(Angel shows one side of the Audience)
                                        both Masters
(Angel shows the other side of the Audience)
                                        and Dames,
    Our service.
(Angel bows. Then showing the 'maidens' across the Audience)

To you, pretty maidens, the same,
(Angel bows)
I come but to say, now all is ended,
We trust that in naught we have offended.
So think no evil, nor chide our play,
But if in aught we have gone astray,
And shown you Worships what was not fit,
Blame not our will,
(Lifting up and letting down his arm as in a 'sorry' gesture)
                      but our lack of wit.
Think it but well, so all's made right—
And we wish you from God Almighty, Good Night.

(Angel and Company bow three times: front, their left, and their right. Angel returns to his/her place and leads the Company through the Audience and out at the back of the Auditorium)

THE COMPANY *(Sing)*
O Man, bethink you how this child,
Of earth nothing afraid,
In Bethlehem born of maiden mild
Was in a stable laid;
Was laid in manger low,
As Holy writ doth show,
Who is the King of all the world
Both now and evermore.

THE END

CHARACTERS IN THE KINGS PLAY

ANGEL: preferably acted by a woman
MARY: young woman
JOSEPH: younger man than in the *Shepherds Play*
BALTHAZZAR: old man
MELCHIOR: middle-aged man
CASPAR: young man
PAGE: young man or woman
VILIGRATIA: old man
HEROD: middle-aged man
LACKEY: young man
PRIESTS (CAIAPHAS, PILATE, JONAS)
CAPTAIN: young man
SOLDIER: middle-aged man
JUDAS: middle-aged man
DEVIL: preferably a man

KINGS PLAY

*The curtains open (see Director's notes 1 and 8), pp. 9 and 10.
All positions and moves are indicated as seen from the Audience.*

(The Company stand on the stage facing the Audience. From left to right: Angel, Mary, Joseph, Balthazzar, Melchior, Caspar, Page, Viligratia, Judas, Herod, Lackey, Captain, Soldier, Caiaphas, Pilate, Jonas, Devil. The three Kings always stand with Melchior in the centre, on his left Balthazzar, and on his right Caspar. Also, when they walk the order is Balthazzar, Melchior, Caspar)

ANGEL *(Goes to the centre of the stage)*
   In right good faith I enter this place.
   God give good evening of his grace,
   A right good evening, the best of cheer,
   The Lord of Heaven
(Angel shows people across the Audience)
                              grant each man here.
   Most reverend Worships,
(Angel shows one side of the Audience)
                              both Master
(Angel shows the other side of the Audience)
                                         and Dame,
   Our service.
(Angel bows. Then showing the 'maidens' across the Audience)
   To you, pretty maidens, the same.
(Angel bows)
   Pray do not grudge or grouch this day
   For one brief hour to hear our play.
   We bring you here no Heathen tale,
   Nor things men gossip o'er their ale,
   Which for your Worships were all unfit,

(Angel makes a 'teaching' gesture)
  But all is ta'en from Holy Writ,
  Namely of the Wise Men three;
  High in the East
(Angel shows the star high above the Audience)
         a Star they see,
  Wherefore a Journey far they go,
(Angel shows people across the Audience)
  As every wise man's son doth know.
  At Jerusalem their steps are stayed.
  To seek that Child out and that Maid;
  Whereat Lord Herod, waxen wroth,
  Chargeth his High Priests, by their troth,
  To search with haste the Scriptures through,
  And of their prophecy tell him true.
(With 'warmth' to the Audience)
  So, would you hear us with good heed,
  Sit still,
(Holds two fingers before mouth)
         and speak no more than need.

(Angel and the Company bow to the Audience: centre, their left, their right. Then Angel goes back to her place and leads the Company, in step, either in silence or with the following music, to their places on the stage, in a clockwise curve)

COMPANY *(Sing)*   Bless, O Lord, the way we tread,
  Bless our coming and our going:
  Bless likewise our daily bread,
  Bless our leaving and our going.
  Bless our death with thy death's leaven
  That to us thy life be given.

(Angel taps his staff and the Company sit down, except the Angel, the Page or the Devil, whoever is to fetch the stool. If it is the Devil, he makes a show of being reluctant to bring the stool—contrary to when he brings Herod's throne—and gets it from the wings, upstage left, drags it across and finally bangs the stool loudly on the

floor. If it is the Page, he brings the stool with reverence and care, from upstage right, goes to Melchior and bows to him. Either way, Melchior rises and goes to the stool in an anticlockwise spiral starting at the back of the stool. Melchior sits, the Page standing on his left.

The Angel goes across the stage, passing in front of Melchior, who suddenly sees the star, and, showing surprise, follows it with his eyes but looking far away above the Audience)

MELCHIOR *(Speaks to the Page)*
Go, Boy, fetch hither my compass and chart,
My globe and the instruments of mine art;
(Page bows, and fetches an optic tube, during which time Melchior meditates)
This star will I essay
That shone not in Heaven before this day—
When Venus with the Sun is conjoined
It augers something new to my mind.
(Page bows and gives the optic tube to Melchior, who looks through it in the direction of the star but higher up)
A dazzling brightness meets my gaze—
This star does fill me with amaze.
So fair a light must needs presage
Some holy thing unto our age.
(He looks again at the star through the tube)
Right in the middle a maid I see
That bears a child upon her knee.
Her forehead, shining clear and bright,
Outdoes that Star and pales its light.
(Angel starts walking towards upstage making a figure of eight, turning at the top of the eight on the words: 'Turns himself unto the East', *and comes back to his place)*
But, see, it moves, it mounts on high,
Swifter and swifter athwart the sky.
The child upon that maiden's breast
Turns himself unto the East.
(Speaks to Page, and gives him back the tube)

Go, Boy fetch hither our mathematician,
To cast this star in its position.
It were much wisdom to unfold
What mean this maid and child of old.

PAGE   Most noble King, I hear and obey
And will fetch Vilagratia hither straightway.
(Bows, fetches Viligratia, bowing to him also. Viligratia goes to Melchior's left and they bow to each other. Page stands behind)

MELCHIOR *(Showing the star)*
This star, what canst thou tell of it?

VILIGRATIA *(Putting his hand above his eyes to look at the star, shows surprise and shakes his head)*
Nothing, O King of mine own wit
(Showing his book)
But if the prophets we read aright,
Great mysteries are brought to light;
As that Esaias hath foretold,
Now I bethink me of prophets old:
(Looks through the book, realizes it is upside down, turns it round, finds the place with his finger and reads)
'In Bethlehem shall a maid give birth,
And her child, the King of
(Shows with his hand up and down)
                    Heaven and Earth.'
(Closes the book in a cloud of dust)

MELCHIOR   Surely that thing the prophet said,
In Bethlehem now is compassed;
Wherefore much vexed am I to know
What gift on him I may bestow.
(Stands up as if inspired)
A heap of **gold** I think to bring,
(Emphasis on 'gold', not on 'heap'!)
For gold is worthiest of a king,

That shall both
(Shows with his hand up and down)
                    Heaven and Earth inherit;
  I trust thereby his grace to merit.
(Speaks to the Page)
  Page, within the hour we part,
  Go, make all ready for the start.
(Speaks to Viligratia)
  Viligratia, as my regent reign
  Till hither I return again.

VILIGRATIA   Most gracious King, as't be thy will,
  I shall this office high fulfil.
(Bows to Melchior)

(They go back to their places on the bench: Melchior, Viligratia and the Page. They walk in step the reverse spiral and sit together simultaneously. Then either Page or Devil moves the stool from the centre to the right of the stage slightly more forward in the same way as for Melchior—the Kings placement of the stool forming a triangle. Balthazzar stands, without Page, and goes in a similar spiral to sit on the stool)

BALTHAZZAR *(Speaking to the Audience)*
  What's this they tell me, that this night
  A wondrous matter is come to light?
  Namely, a star most bright and clear
  Wherein a maiden doth appear,
  All with a King
(Shows with his hand down and up)
                    of Earth and Heaven,
  A tender child, both young and fair,
  A child most wonderful, most rare—
  To him must incense needs be given.
(He gets up and takes a step forward)
  This star, this child, this King to greet
  Now step I out into the street.

Pray, is this thing to others known
   That unto me my folk have shown?
(He looks far above the Audience and discovers the star)
   O wonder, the like I ne'er heard tell
   In saga nor in chronicle.
   Maid and Mother was none I guess,
   Nor child king, rich yet penniless.
(Angel walks another figure of eight)
   To Bethlehem beckons us this star—
   Then follow, though the way be far.
   I know not well on learned ground
   This mystery's thesis to expound:
   A child that lieth in a stall
   Shall be the King of Jewry all.
   Wherefore with daybreak let me rise,
   And find that child out where he lies.

(Balthazzar too walks the spiral back to his place on the bench and sits down. Page or Devil changes the stool once more to the third point of the triangle. If the Devil, he looks as if he is going to bang the stool but, just before the stool touches the floor, he slows down and puts it quietly down, mocking silently the Audience)

CASPAR *(Caspar—the young King—walks with more determination the same spiral and just stands in front of the stool. He sees the star immediately in the same position as did the other two Kings)*
   O wonder rare, O highest bliss,
   The very time fulfilled it is
   That born should be Messiah child
   And of a maiden undefiled.
(Angel walks the same figure of eight)
   See, the star doth call us hence
   Homage to do, and reverence,
   And thoroughly maketh us to know
   All the prophets did foreshow.
   With brightest beams it becks us on

To find that Mother and that Son.
Since he is King
(Shows with his hand up and down)
            of Heaven and Earth
Myrrh must be offered at his birth.
With such oblation to commend me
I trust to win him to befriend me.

(Caspar too walks the same spiral back to his place on the bench and sits own. Angel walks back to the front of the Company and stands on stage right. Page, or Devil, takes the stool back. Angel taps his/her staff, whereupon the Company rise and sing, going anticlockwise through the Audience, across the stage and back to their places on the bench)

COMPANY *(Sing)*
   Shine star and light the Wisemen's way,
   The King of Heaven and Earth this day
   Is to our world descended.
   And wise men seeking for a king
   Where learnt ye this last secret thing,
   Whence came this wisdom splendid?
   Follow, follow
   From lands afar,
   O'er hill and hollow
   Follow the star
   To the stall where the child is tended.

(Angel taps his/her staff and the Company sit simultaneously except for the three Kings and Page. Angel walks to front stage left followed by Melchior and Page. Page, attracted by 'noises', overtakes the King and looks to the right side of the stage, whilst Melchior stops and Angel continues to walk and finally stands on the left)

PAGE   Most gracious king, a noise I hear,
   A rout of folk is riding near.

Me'seems that on a King they stay
Who freely will direct our way.

MELCHIOR   Withdraw, and leave me here alone
While to these strangers I make me known.
(Page goes back to his place on the bench. Balthazzar and Caspar, passing behind Melchior, walk a curve and end up on either side of him)
Greetings, good friends,
(They all three bow together)
                          pray whither bound
With such stout hearts, thus richly found?

BALTHAZZAR   Our loves to you, Sir:
(They bow again)
                          but whither go ye
And all your noble company?

MELCHIOR   We thank your loves, and do intend
To Jerusalem our journey's end.

CASPAR   To that same city we too repair,
Then tell us, pray, what make you there?

MELCHIOR   'Tis clear to read in Esaiay
A child shall be upon a day,
In Bethlehem shall be his birth
That is the King
(Shows with his hand up and down)
                          of Heaven and Earth.
But now a marvel it is to learn—
(He shows the star high above the Audience—but in the direction of the star on the staff—and they all look)
So bright a star in Heaven doth burn
That, wot you well, this very morn,
That child and King is truly born.

BALTHAZZAR   Of very truth I may you tell
  To us that self-same thing befell.
(Shows the star same as before, and they all look at it)
  A star before our gaze shone clear
  Wherein did maid and child appear.
  Surely this day hath brought to light
  What heathen times long hid from sight.

CASPAR   Sirs, this is fallen in marvellous sort,
  Me, too,
(Shows the star same as before, and they all look at it)
        this star hath hither brought.
  To find that child is all our passion—
  Then must we stir in busy fashion.

(Angel starts walking in a curve behind the Kings so that he is right in the middle of the curve on Melchior's words 'friends'. He arrives on the left side of Balthazzar on the words 'on our road' to lead them in the next song)

MELCHIOR   The star doth like a beacon shine
  Riding before us for a sign.
  Yet nothing of the road we know
  And must no means of help forego.
  Friends,
(They take a step towards each other)
        since in such a case we stand,
  Strangers here in a strange land,
  I counsel that we turn aside,
  And to Jerusalem city ride,
  These tidings there to noise abroad
  And seek guidance on our road.

(Angel leads the Kings in a figure of eight on the stage, and takes them to their places on the bench)

ANGEL, THREE KINGS *(Sing)*
  Three Kings a-leading and what led them?

A star that stood o'er Bethlehem,
Over a stable
And over a cradle.

(Angel and the Kings stand in front of their places. Angel taps his staff and the Company rise simultaneously. They sing going anti-clockwise through the Audience, and go back to their places on the bench. Angel taps his staff and they all sit simultaneously, except for Devil who goes in the front left wing to fetch Herod's throne)

COMPANY *(Sing)*
Three wise men in King Herod's days
From Eastern lands they took their ways
As to Jerusalem they came
The Christ was born in Bethlehem.

Then asked they of low and high
Where that newborn King should lie,
Among the Jews by prophets old
Clearly unto us foretold.

(From the front stage left Devil brings the 'heavy' throne, pulling and pushing, placing it as far forward as possible on the left side, almost in the centre. He cleans it, making a lot of fuss, spits on it to shine it and sits on it as if he is a king, until he suddenly sees the Audience and 'remembers' that he must fetch Herod. He goes to Herod and gives him an exaggerated bow. Herod and Lackey stand up; Herod goes to his throne and sits down. Lackey stands to Herod's right—he looks half asleep)

HEROD *(To the Audience)* I am the King of all this land,
God help me if I slack my hand!
Acclaimed by my people all
Lord spiritual and temporal,
Acknowledged by the Jewish moot
Omnipotent King, Lord absolute.
This day a judgment seat I hold

Wherein I judge both young and old,
They throng in crowds our council room
To see our state and hear their doom.
(The Kings stand up)
So, let them grovel on the floor—

(Melchior taps his sceptre and Herod is frightened and Lackey 'wakes up' and shows fear of Herod)
Who's that who knocks upon the door?

LACKEY *(Bows to Herod and runs towards the Kings, turning outwards and making a curve behind Herod. He stops short and looks carefully at the Kings as if they are some distance away, then runs back the same way, bows to Herod and speaks excitedly, but with fear of Herod)*
Most gracious King, here is a press,
'Twere hard to know their business.
Much Lords and Kings are in their throng,
With splendid garb they pace along,
Majestic is their port.
(Suddenly more worried and frightened)
     God send
They come not here for evil end.

HEROD Go, ask of them what is their mind
And what from us they look to find.

LACKEY *(Bows to Herod and goes the same way right up to the Kings. He bows to the Kings but still looks frightened)*
King Herod greets your Lordships well,
Of your intent he would hear tell,
What blood ye are, and from what land,
And what ye look for at his hand.

MELCHIOR *(Takes a step forward, and Lackey is more frightened)*
Of kingly stem we all are born,
Two are from Saba,

(He indicates himself and Balthazzar, who takes a step forward. Lackey is more frightened again, and counts on his fingers as the Kings are presented. He keeps his three fingers up until he speaks to Herod)
                      the third from Morn.
(Lackey again more frightened)
    King Herod's self we fain would greet,
    And with his favour trust to meet.
(Lackey bows and rushes back the same way, still holding up his three fingers)

LACKEY *(Bows to Herod, still holding his fingers up; he speaks as if he has learnt by heart what the King has said)*
    Of kingly stem they all are born,
(Counts on the fingers he has kept holding up)
    Two are from Saba, the third from Morn.
    King Herod's self they fain would greet,
    And with his favour trust to meet.

HEROD   Escort them hither. We are at leisure,
    And grant them audience at our pleasure.
(Lackey bows to Herod and runs back to Kings, and bows. Whilst waiting for the Kings, Herod stands up)

LACKEY   The King your presence doth beseech
    And with your Lordships would fain have speech
(Makes a gesture to show Herod and bows. He goes back to his place near Herod. The Kings move together towards Herod. They all bow)

HEROD   Welcome my Lords. What would ye of me,
    That hither you ride from far country?

CASPAR   Your kingly love we fain would win
    To hear our journey's origin.
    In Saba, in our land afar,
    Rose in the East a wondrous star,

Wherein a maid a child did bear—
(Herod, as the speech progresses shows surprise, then becomes worried and angry)
　　Mark well, O King, what you do hear:
　　Whereat we marvelled much with mirth,
　　And said, Messiah is born on earth.
　　A child he shall hold kingly sway
　　And all the Jews shall him obey.
　　Him now to seek with eager care,
　　Unto your court, O King, we fare.

HEROD *(Speaking to himself)*
　　What? In my land can such things be,
　　And known to strangers and not to me?
(To the Kings with pretended warmth)
　　Sirs, get you gone to Bethlehem straight,
　　And find that child and King algate,
　　And when ye have done him reverence,
　　Return, and hither tidings bring—
　　We too would bring an offering;
(To himself with venom)
　　A kingly gift we shall devise.
(To the Kings)
　　This do with speed and enterprise,
　　And win much favour in our eyes.

CASPAR　　Great King, fear not to find us slack
　　To bring hot-haste our tidings back.

(They all bow, and Herod sits down brooding. The Kings move to the right. Angel gets up and walks towards the Kings so that he/she is beside Balthazzar on his words 'first 'gan know')

MELCHIOR　　To horse! To horse
　　To Jerusalem take we now our course.

BALTHAZZAR *(Discovering the star, looking far ahead above the Audience to his left)*

See, it moves athwart the sky,
The star that erst we did espy,
In our eastern land aglow,
Whereby that child we first 'gan know.

(Angel leads the Kings to their places on the bench, in a figure of eight, with music)

HEROD   This news doth move me to fear and anger,
Being no true King here but a stranger,
Go, lackey,
(Lackey 'wakes up' and shows fear of Herod)
            fetch some learned priest,
I will ask him of this star in the East,
This King the Jews must needs obey—
Go, fetch a High Priest here straightway.

LACKEY *(Frightened of Herod, he exaggerates)*
Most gracious King, I hear and obey,
Instanter will I ride away,
From every corner of the land,
To fetch a High Priest to your hand.

(Herod, impatient, bangs his sceptre on the throne and Lackey jumps and runs to fetch the three Priests on the bench, then he sits down on the bench. The Priests stand up and make a great fuss in bowing and greeting each other, and finally approach Herod with great fear. They stand on Herod's left: Caiaphas, Pilate and Jonas. They bow to him and show their fear by shaking their hands by the side of their heads and repeating each other's and Herod's words—see underlined words as examples. Devil stands up and hovers at the back, listening to the scene)

CAIAPHAS   Lord Herod, Caiaphas am I,
Would never give my King a lie;
But I must say you <u>such a thing</u>,
Such a thing, my <u>sweetest King</u>,

And if your Majesty will promise
To bear Caiaphas no malice

HEROD Say on, Sir, nor our anger fear,
Though little pleasure it is to hear;
Nor will we not our malice wreak,
Seeing we called you here to speak,
But if of prophecy ought you would
(Priests repeat 'prophecy' several times with awe and worry)
See that it is of omen good.

CAIAPHAS Great King, this speak I in your ear,
Thus the palmist singeth clear,
David's son shall think no scorn
In Judah's Bethlehem to be born.
His sons shall swallow up his foes,
And vanquish all who him oppose.
Much folk shall follow him on earth
And be blessed in his birth.
His name shall be Emmanuel
So prophesieth Ezekiel,
(Speaks faster and faster and the other priests join in. They all stamp one foot on 'feet')
Butter and honey shall he eat,
Good and right he shall entreat,
But evil set beneath his feet.

HEROD But how may be a thing so rare
As that a maid a child should bear?

CAIAPHAS *(Lifts one hand and speaks as if reciting)*
The seed of the woman shall bruise the serpent's head,
What was lost he shall find, and his life shall quicken the dead.

HEROD A neighbour King hath sought me out,
And counselled me beyond a doubt,

And said: In Bethlehem this morn
A Saviour to the world is born.
A righteous prince, a shepherd true,
That all men give him homage due.
O King, said he, stop not thine ear
But ponder well what thou dost hear.
If this be true, 'twere plain to see
My crown stands much in jeopardy.

CAIAPHAS   O Sire, it were a petty tale
To think (ha ha!) your realm should fail!
A King he shall be called, pardy,
But wield less power than a flea.
(They show the Roman gesture of a thumb down)
Condemned to die a death of shame,
All men shall curse his people's name.

HEROD   Methinks it were the better way,
While he is young to put him away.

PILATE   Sweet Sovereign, set your mind at ease
Nor let this bubble fret your peace,
Until the wise men homeward bound
Say truly whether thus 'twas found.

HEROD   Much fear we lest these tidings ride
Already through the countryside.
For yester e'en (so were we told)
While shepherds watched upon the wold
Sudden an Angel them beforn
Proclaimed a King was newly born.
Sir Caiaphas, say, upon what ground
Shall this newborn King be found
To whom the Jews shall do service?
What can your prophets tell of this?

(Caiaphas pushes Jonas forward to answer instead of him and gives him the scroll he had in his belt. Jonas is reluctant and resists.

In the scuffle Jonas drops the scroll, picks it up, etc. and finally goes up to Herod, the other two behind him)

JONAS *(Reading from the scroll)*
   All prophets with one voice maintain
   Christ the King is <u>without stain,</u>
   In <u>Bethlehem</u> he shall be born
   That lieth in <u>Judea's land</u>
   Thereto all <u>prophets</u> do set their hand.
(They all put their right hands together)

HEROD   Right!
   Enough and plenty for tonight!
   Be off,
(The priests start running towards their places on the bench, then stop to listen to Herod)
         and make of this no chatter
(The priests repeat 'no chatter' several times, making a racket, then stop to listen once more to Herod)
   Myself will undertake this matter.
(Knowing what Herod is capable of, they throw up their hands in horror and run to their places on the bench. They are so upset that they bump into the bench, which falls down. They pick it up and sit down simultaneously, suddenly completely still.

   During the next part of Herod's speech the Devil comes gradually forward in an S-shaped line so that he is near Herod on the words 'O woe, O woe'. He mimics Herod throughout. Herod now rises and paces about)
   I'll work my wits, I'll stir about,
   I'll let the young knave's life blood out!
(Devil laughs loudly and nastily)
   Ah! How the Devil laughs this day
   To see me cast my soul away.
   What? Must King Herod plead and cry?
   Far better curse my fate and die.
   What other can I do or say?
   Will no one be my help this day?

(He sits on his throne and holds it)
   Robbed of my throne, bereft of friend,
   I wait my miserable end.
(Speaking to the Audience)
   Will no one do poor Herod right?
(He looks up)
   No God?
(To the Audience)
           No Man?
(Devil is now behind the throne and shows himself to one side of Herod. Herod looks to that side with the next words, but Devil has already gone to the other side)
                No Fiend?
(Repeat to the other side)
                        No Sprite?
   But out, alas, of all forsook,
   Whither for friendship can I look?
   O woe! O woe!

DEVIL *(Echoing Herod's 'O woe! O woe!')*   O Ho, O Ho,
   What makes you here with moan and groan?
   Here's one leaves not his friends alone.
   Say on, what is this direful need?

HEROD *(In a complaining voice)*
   For very fear I die indeed
   That in Judea a King is born,
   And I, of every friend forlorn,
   Ah me, poor devil, what shall I do?

DEVIL   Peace, peace I am a devil too,
   And devil must by devil stand.
   Pluck up your courage, man.
(He offers his hand)
                        My hand
(Herod puts his hand reluctantly in Devil's hand. Devil grabs it)
   To see you safely through this thing.

Together we will have this King.
Trust me to counsel what's to do,
I am no more his friend than you.
(Devil whispers in Herod's ear)
   Arm, King, and strike—make no delay.

HEROD *(Brooding and then more and more agitated)*
   So many, partner, must I slay?
   Not one alone, but score on score?
   For my own skin I tremble sore.
   For such evil, alack! alack!
   In my own coin they'll pay me back,
   I fear for this they'll see me dead.

DEVIL   Pish! Put this nonsense from your head.
   What, would you be a devil, Sir King?
   Hark now, I have the very thing.
   All little childer of two year old,
   Or under, get them in your hold—
   Child or Mother, you shall spare none,
   Born or unborn, all is one—
   And when you get them in your noose
(Devil jumps for joy and speaks to the Audience)
   Ha! how the fox will maul the goose
   My cronies must not miss this joke!
(Gradually exiting from upstage left, stepping on time to the rhythm of the words: 'rag and bag goes old Nick Nack')
   Rag and bag, goes old Nick Nack
(Stops and speaks to the Audience before exiting)
   To fetch his fellows on his back!

(Herod rises and runs back to his place on the bench, looking afraid and sits down. Devil comes out of the wing downstage left and removes the throne. Angel taps his staff, the Company rise, whilst Devil joins them and they sing standing still)

COMPANY *(Sing)*
   With God we fain would tune our song again.

Whilst Herod now doth arm his hand,
Onward the three Kings ride
The star that is their guide
O'er Bethlehem stays, and still doth stand.

(Angel leads the Company anticlockwise through the Audience, then across the stage and back to their places on the bench)

COMPANY *(Sing)*   A Child is born in Bethlehem,
This year, this year,
Wherefore exult Jerusalem,
This year we joy and sing.
We sing the Mother of our Lord,
And Jesus her sweet boy,
And Christ we sing above all thing
This year with mirth and joy.

Now lies he in a manger small,
This year, this year,
Would shall at last be Lord of all,
This year we joy and sing.
We sing the Mother of our Lord,
And Jesus her sweet boy,
And Christ we sing above all thing
This year with mirth and joy.

(The Angel taps his/her staff and the Company sit down simultaneously except for Angel and Page. The Page goes to fetch Mary's stool from the upstage right wing, and places it stage left—same place as in the Shepherd's Play. Mary and Joseph stand up and Joseph leads Mary to the stool. Mary sits down. Lights dim more, so that the left side of the stage is in the dark. Melchior taps his sceptre, and the three Kings rise simultaneously. Angel starts walking, leading the three Kings and turning to go upstage. Then Angel turns back, in a curve, to come forward and goes to his/her right to stop on downstage left, in the dark. When the Kings come forward, they go to their left and to the front of the stage, where the spotlight comes on Caspar)

CASPAR *(Taking another step forward)*   O Lord, I pray
Forsake us not,
Lighten our eyes in this great need,
That we die not the death. O lead,
Lead us, Lord, the narrow way
That we stumble not, nor stray,
But walk as ever in thy light.

MELCHIOR   Here are two ways, which is the right?

(Angel starts walking towards Mary and Joseph and stops behind them. Lights grow slightly brighter on them)

BALTHAZZAR *(Turns and sees the star above Mary)*
See, see, the star doth stop and stay,
To yonder stall make we our way
(Balthazzar leads the Kings to Mary and Joseph; they bow)
God greet you, maiden without peer,
Surely the Child we seek lies here?

MARY *(Sings)*   The Child ye seek ye have surely found
In swaddling clothes all meanly bound.

(The lights come up. The three Kings bow to Mary and retrace their steps and stand on the right front stage)

MELCHIOR   Come then,
Our gifts to offer make we bold
Myrrh, frankincense and the red red gold.

(Music is played and during the music Page rises and comes forward to collect the sceptres. Page bows in front of each King in turn, starting with Balthazzar, then takes the sceptre and bows again. He then goes to the next King and repeats the same until he has taken the three sceptres. He takes them off stage in the wing, where he gets the first gift for Balthazzar. He bows to the King, gives him the gift, bows again, then goes back to the wing to fetch

the next gift, etc.—gold for Melchior, incense for Balthazzar and myrrh for Caspar. When he has finished he goes to sit on his place on the bench)

MELCHIOR *(Takes a step forward so that he is the apex of a triangle, and sings)*
 Psallite unigenito
 Christo, dei filio,
 Psallite redemptori
 Domino puerulo
 Jacenti in praesepio
(Melchior steps back)

BALTHAZZAR   Now which of us shall be the first?

CASPAR *(To Balthazzar)*
 Sir, you are the eldest here, I wis,
 Wherefore to you this honour is,
 Enter, and we will come behind,
 So seems it best unto my mind.

BALTHAZZAR *(To Melchior)*
 The honour is yours, Sir, by kingly use.

MELCHIOR   I will this honour not refuse,
 In God's name, then, I enter here,
 And to this Child I bring new year.

(The Kings go to Mary and Joseph, in step, in the following order: Melchior, Caspar and Balthazar. They stand in a diagonal, with Balthazzar furthest away from the Child, holding their gifts)

MELCHIOR *(Kneels and puts his gift down on the floor in front of him)*
 Blest be thou, Child, and blest thy Dame,
 And blest be God I hither came,

A journey far we needs have made
To find this place where thou are laid.
(Picks up his gift)
   I pray thee, and I give this gold,
   That for thy friend thou wilt me hold.
(Puts the gift down in front of Mary and speaks to Mary and Joseph)
   Friends, treat this Child with honour due,
   And rear ye him as parents true.
   Nothing for tears hast thou, sweet boy,
   And of my gifts I wish thee joy.
(Brings his hands together in a gesture of prayer or reverence and bows his head)

CASPAR *(Kneels and puts his gift down on the floor in front of him)*
   All hail, great King and Hero great,
   Though meanly here thou keep'st thy state,
   Here have we sought thee in a shed—
   Not so a King should make his bed.
   A star hath hither been my guide,
   O King, and homeward when I ride
   Each hour, I'll think upon thee, yea,
   Thy praise be in my mouth alway
   Till all the world shall know thy worth.
(Picks up his gift)
   Take here the sweetness of the earth,
   Myrrh, gathered in my eastern land,
   Whereby I give me to thy hand.
(Puts the gift down in front of Mary and brings his hands together in a gesture of prayer or reverence and bows his head)

BALTHAZZAR *(Kneels and puts his gift down on the floor in front of him)*
   Now come I too, thou Kingly Grace,
   Thou Hero, born of royal race,
   For thee with heart and soul I yearn,

Before my steps thy star did burn.
(Picks up his gift)
This incense for my gift I bring
Which doth befit one born a King.
(Puts the gift down in front of Mary)
Sire, if hereafter I come to thee,
I pray receive me graciously.
(Brings his hands together in a gesture of prayer or reverence and bows his head)

JOSEPH   Most worthy Sirs, God give you meed,
That sought us out and in sore need
With gifts did comfort our poor state,
In Heaven your reward is great.

MARY *(Sings)*   Sirs, for your gifts and love this day,
Our love and thanks be yours alway,
Be blest in what this night has showed,
And with fresh courage take your road.

(The Kings rise, bow to the Child, then to Mary and then to Joseph)

CASPAR   Now farewell, Joseph, goodman friend,
Be zealous still this Child to tend,
For him nor toil nor trouble spare;
The Lord himself reward your care.

BALTHAZZAR *(Makes a blessing gesture)*
Now God, the everlasting Lord,
From fear and danger be thy ward.

(The Kings go back to their former places on the front stage right. Music is played whilst Page comes forwards and gives back the sceptres, starting with Caspar in the same way as before. Then, he goes back to his place on the bench)

MELCHIOR   To Herod next our steps are bound
   To tell him where this Child be found—
(The lights dim)
   But Sirs, the darkness falls apace,
   Needs must we couch us in this place.

THREE KINGS *(Sing)*   Upon a night I lay and slept.
(They kneel down, bow their heads and rest them on their upright sceptres)

(Angel goes to the Kings, walking a curve at the back of the stage, and stands behind them. Spotlight on Angel)

ANGEL   You Holy Kings from Orient,
   Of God Almighty am I sent
   That unto you I should reveal
   Great peril treadeth at your heel.
   Get you not home the selfsame way
   Lest Herod shall you take and slay,
   Who secretly doth hide his wroth;
   God shall show you another path.
(Angel exits upstage right, spotlight on him dims. Then general lights come up and the Kings wake up and stand)

MELCHIOR   A marvellous dream here have I heard,
   An angel stayed me with a word,
   That Herod's house we should pass by
   And home another way should hie,
   For in his raging he hath sworn
   To do to death this Child new-born.

BALTHAZZAR
   This selfsame dream I too have dreamed;
   An angel warned us, so meseemed,
   That Herod worketh wit and will,
   The lifeblood of this Child to spill—
   But, an thou plann'st this devilry,
   Herod, thou gett's no help from me.

(As they sing, Balthazzar leads the Kings clockwise in front of the Audience and back on the stage to their places on the bench. Melchior taps his staff and they sit down simultaneously)

THREE KINGS *(Sing)*
    Balthazzar King rides over the hill,
    He hath found the Child and wrought his will,
    Hath wrought, hath wrought his will.

(The lights dim and Mary and Joseph look asleep, Joseph resting his head on his staff. Then Angel enters from upstage right and goes to Joseph. Spotlight on Angel)

ANGEL   Joseph, Joseph,
(Joseph lifts his head and listens)
                              mark you well,
    Good soul, the word I shall you tell
    From God who hath me hither sped,
    Rise, Joseph, make not here your bed,
    Rise, man, take wife and child by hand
    And get you straight to Egypt land,
    Nor to Judea back return
    Till of this matter more you learn.

(Angel exits upstage right from the Audience while the spotlight on him/her dims. Joseph goes back to sleep. Then the general lights come up and Mary and Joseph wake up)

JOSEPH   And must we fare abroad this night?
    Ah, grievous, grievous is our plight—
    To Egypt land how shall we go
    When nothing of the road we know,
    While savage beasts beset the way
    And prowling robbers stalk their prey,
    And 'tis a mighty way to ride?

MARY *(Sings)*   God will surely be our guide
    And lead us rightly on the way,

Nor suffer his own folk to stray.
His angel with us he will send
And bring us surely to the end.
(Stands up)
Come then, make ready with good heart,
Saddle the ass, 'tis time to part.

(They take a few steps, then they stop and Joseph turns towards the 'stable')

JOSEPH   Dear house, God have thee in his care,
I shall not find thy like elsewhere.
But 'tis God's will I should thee leave,
His first commandment to achieve.

MARY *(Sings)*   Farewell, we may no more abide,
To Egypt's land we needs must ride.

(Joseph leads Mary, in step, to their places on the bench. They sit down simultaneously. Devil gets up and fetches Herod's throne, which he pushes and drags and cleans as before. On the throne are some steps, which the Devil installs behind the throne, making it obvious, and a purse, which he shakes to hear the coins in it. Then he gets Herod and this time shows him the throne by an irreverent gesture of his thumb over his shoulder. Herod gets up and goes to stand in front of the throne. Lackey goes to his place and the Captain and Soldier go to stand on Herod's left, the Captain nearest to Herod. Devil hovers at the back listening)

HEROD   What though I plotted had and planned,
And with my sly and cunning hand
Made ready a right royal feast
To greet these Kings from out the East,
And this Sir Child they do revere,
Yet, in my bones I have a fear
They did beguile me and betray
And robbed poor Herod of his prey.

(He paces from side to side, the Devil imitating him)
   I think and think and think again
   How best to set this thing in train,
   And when I have him in my net
   What gift from me 'twere best to get.
   Full subtly will I go to work,
   Like fox that in the hedge doth lurk,
   While all his heart and sense is set
   Some fat goose in his maw to get.
   As crafty as a cat i' the house
   I'll be, that hears a wainscot mouse.
(Devil comes forward and whispers in Herod's ear, then exits upstage left)
   And now I have it, by good hap,
   A plan this infant to entrap—
(Sitting on the bench, Mary crosses her arms over her chest, stands up and walks slowly a curve on the stage, at the back, but towards Herod, so that she arrives on the words 'inheritance remain' on the stage front left)
   With my all-conquering warrior band
   All babes I'll get into my hand,
   And though their mothers 'murder' cry
   And scream the sky down, what care I?—
   So that my realm I do maintain
(Sits on his throne)
   And my inheritance remain.

(Mary walks across the stage in front of Herod, singing. He is transfixed and puts his arm across his face, palm out as if wanting to protect himself from this vision)

MARY *(Sings)*   Great King, to Mercy mend your mind
   Lest grief come suddenly behind;
   If so much guiltless blood you shed
   What call you, King, on your own head?
(Mary goes back to her place on the bench and sits down, forming the gesture of holding the Child as before)

HEROD *(Jumping out of his throne and making a gesture as if he wants to get rid of Mary)*
    Out of my sight, thou prating witch,
    What! Thinkest thou a king to teach?
    I tell thee, I lose both life and crown,
    If not this wickedness be put down.
    It were no monarch, but a hind
    Would let a scold's tongue rule his mind.
(Devil brings a scroll, from stage left down and gives it to Herod who takes it not seeing him. Devil goes back in the wing)
    Sir Knave!
(Captain takes a step forward)
             You have your orders plain,
    What each must do, you and your train.
    Take then our royal decree, whereto
    We set our sign and seal.
(He stamps the scroll with his sceptre)
                  This do,
    And publish it in every town,
    Take it, Sir,
(Gives the scroll to Captain)
             cry it up and down
    'Whereas King Herod'—cry it fair—
    'And who fulfils not this command
    Shall forfeit life and goods and lands.'

CAPTAIN *(Bows to Herod, comes as far forward as possible, opens the scroll and reads loudly and proudly from it)*
    Let all take notice of this decree.
(Judas gets up and comes forward listening with one hand around his ear. During the Captain's speech he stops in front of the Captain on the right)
    Whereas his puissant majesty
    King Herod, our rightful sovereign lord,
    Hath given order that by the sword
    All little children
(Gets more interested and begins to worry)

of two years old,
(Gets even more worried and now frightened)
Or under, we bring them to his hold.
(Pulls himself together and speaks the rest loudly)
Be it known, sans favour and sans fear,
None shall escape for gold nor gear,
And who fulfils not this command
Shall forfeit life and goods and lands.

JUDAS   Woe's me, the cruel bloody deed!
(Speaks to Herod)
Certes to thee our lives are feed.
But must our pretty babes be slain?
Nought comes of this but grief and pain.

HEROD   The guilt of this shall rest on thee.
(Speaks to the Captain)
Go, put him under lock and key.

CAPTAIN *(Takes Judas by his collar and speaks to him)*
Thou villain, wouldst revile the King?
I tell thee for this thou'lt surely swing.
Far better a few children slain,
Than all of us dead like rats in a drain.

(Captain drags Judas across the stage in front of Herod and exits stage front left. In the wings Judas gives a loud cry which is interrupted suddenly)

HEROD *(Very frightened by the cry)*
Run lackey, run with cry and hue,
Bring me my trusty Captain true.
(Lackey runs to fetch the Captain. They both go back to their places by Herod's side. Same as with the scroll the Devil passes a sword to Herod, who does not see him. Devil goes back in the wing)

Look you, Captain, you have your sword—
Four thousand men attend your word—
Out with them, harry house and hall,
And strangle me all young children small.
On pain of death no bribe receive,
Nor pity move thee, one child to leave.
Slaughter them, every mother's son,
No rest till all to death be done.
(Takes the purse and gives it to the Captain)
For this henceforth draw double pay
In coins of gold of good assay.

CAPTAIN *(Takes the purse from the throne and is excited by the gold)*
All it has pleased my gracious Sire
To vouchsafe to his servant's ear,
(Though all unworthy) with joy I heard
Nor failed to comprehend each word:
And will fulfil in every part
With all the sinews of my heart.
(Steps as far forward as possible and speaks to the Audience)
Ha! would they were already here,
Those little childer of two year!
(Gets more and more out of control as he speaks, swinging his sword, until Herod has enough and bangs his sceptre on the throne to bring the Captain back to order after the word 'a goodly beast')
My trusty sword would not be long
To make them sing a merry song.
My heart leaps up, I laugh, I shout,
To see the red blood gushing out,
I carol, as for some holy feast
Where men kill many a goodly beast.
(Steps back)
Forward! Thus march out to the town
To put this foul rebellion down.
Long live King Herod!
(Walks across in front of Herod, and stops to speak to Lackey)

> Lackey, run,
> And see with me this work begun.

LACKEY   With all my strength I'll hew and hack,
In work like this I'll not be slack.

CAPTAIN   Ha! Such I seek, good men and true,
To quit themselves as men should do!
(To Herod)
Lord King, be still of courage stout,
We'll make the children's blood gush out.

(The Captain leads, the Soldier goes across in front of Herod to join him, the Lackey follows the Soldier and they all exit the stage through the left front wing. Lights dim. Company rise together, and throw their hands up in horror, looking towards the left side of the stage; then they let their arms fall in despair and bow their heads and sit down again simultaneously and slowly. Lights come up slightly, and Captain enters and speaks to Herod. He looks sickened and desperate)

CAPTAIN   *(Speaks slowly)*
Most puissant Sire, give gracious heed
And hearken to thy servant's deed.
I with my single hand have slain
One hundred thousand, twenty and twain.
So be you still of courage stout—
We've made the children's blood gush out.
(Goes across, behind the throne to his place)

SOLDIER   *(Enters very excited and proud)*
Eighty thousand is my sum
That I have sent to kingdom come.
(Mimics what he says)
The last small brat I plucked from bed,
And 'here comes a chopper' I chuckled and said—
Then out with my sword and chopped off his head.
(Goes across behind Herod to his place)

LACKEY *(Enters very proud)*
  Most gracious King, now be it said
  What I this day have compassed.
  Two thousands have I put to rest,
  And hushed them at their mothers' breast.
  (Goes across behind Herod to stand next to the Soldier)

HEROD   My thanks, good knaves. For this deed's sake
  One half my realm and riches take.
(The Captain, Soldier and Lackey bow, go to the bench and sit simultaneously)

(Devil enters from upstage left, carrying a bag on his shoulder and throws it down at Herod's feet. Herod is very frightened)

DEVIL   More company, King, here's Nick come back,
  And brought his children in a sack.
(Opens the bag and takes little black puppets and puts them one by one on Herod. Herod recoils from each puppet. When all the puppets are out, the Devil looks frantically into the bag)
  Curse them, young devils—if you please,
(He picks up the puppets again and puts them back in the bag. Then he throws the bag on the floor and in a tantrum stamps on it several times)
  They've picked my pockets and filched the cheese.
  But they shan't have bread—not a scrap of the worst,
(Puts the bag back on his shoulder)
  Curse them, I'll see them in—
(Pauses and speaks to the Audience, indicating 'Heaven' above, but not looking up)
                    Heaven first.
(Exits upstage left. Lackey and Captain, the latter still looking dispirited, come forward and go to their places)

CAPTAIN   Most gracious Majesty, be it known
  We have searched the city up and down,
  And scanned and scoured the countryside,

Hour by hour, both far and wide;
Yet search you may both high and low,
Of newborn king there's naught to show;
(Herod stands up slowly and very tense. Captain speaks with renewed pathos)
But all small children of years twain
At thy behest we them have slain.
Thy servants wrought what thou hast willed,
And in this hour it stands fulfilled.
(Goes back to his place on the bench)

HEROD *(In a rage)*
Not found? Not found? Then by this hand
The felon child is fled the land.
Now dead am I, with anguish torn,
To think another God is born—
(Walks from side to side)
I'll find him out, what e'er befall,
Ah, were it at Bethlehem in a stall?
(Feels faint and sits on his throne)
Aye me, my spirit faints this day,
And all my life blood ebbs away.
(His head falls backwards; his crown falls to the floor)

LACKEY *(Hysterical and worried)*
Bring here an apple and a knife,
With sweets to save my dear lord's life.

(Devil passes him an apple with a dagger through it. Lackey gives it to Herod, who has no strength left and drops it to the floor. Angel comes forward from the upstage centre wing and goes up on the step behind the throne, holding behind his back a crown of flame in his left hand. As he sings he lowers his staff slowly by Herod's side, until the star almost touches the floor)

ANGEL *(Sings)*   Herod, Herod cruel King,
Thou hast done what wicked thing!

For thou didst the children slay,
Death shall throw at thee this day.

HEROD *(Weakly)*   A cloud of light. What can it mean?
A plot against my life, I ween.
Run, lackey, run, with cry and hue
Bring me my trusty Captain true.
(Lackey runs to fetch the Captain and the Soldier. They come together worried, and stand all three to the left of Herod: Captain nearest to Herod, then Soldier and Lackey)
Look you, Captain, this sceptre take
Whereby my promised gift I make,
(Gives the sceptre to Captain. Captain, Soldier and Lackey look at it fascinated)
It hath confounded me all my day
Whereby the devil hath led me astray,
For this to Abraham's garden I fare.
(His head falls back again in a faint)

ANGEL   Ye devils,
*(Devil enters, **wearing wings**, from the front stage left)*
lead him to your lair,
Long time on earth he hath served you well,
Take him home to your nest in Hell,
Wrap him in robes of royal red,
And set
(With a large gesture, puts the crown of fire on Herod's head)
Hell's crown upon his head.
(Herod sits up holding his head. The Angel lifts the star, goes down the stairs and turning round goes back upstage and exits through the centre)

CAPTAIN, SOLDIER, LACKEY *(Speaking together)*
What helps the sceptre now
Or crown upon the brow?
Sceptre and crown and sway
All have at last their day.

(They throw the sceptre on the floor and go, looking dispirited, to sit down on the bench. Herod gets up as if he wants to 'escape'. The Devil springs forward and forces Herod back on his throne. The following dialogue mounts in a crescendo)

DEVIL   Down, Sir, down.
   What hast so soon devoured the fat,
   And left thy vomit on the mat?

HEROD   O devil, let me longer live
   And a pair of black oxen I will thee give.

DEVIL   None of them,
   I will have thee.

HEROD   O devil, let me longer live
   And a pair of black horses I will thee give

DEVIL   None of them,
   I will have thee.

HEROD *(Falls on his knees, begging)*
   O devil, let me longer live
   And half my kingdom I will thee give

DEVIL   What need we bandy wordes moe?
   Art not mine, come weal, come woe?
   With me must dwell
   In pains of Hell—
(To the Audience)
   And some others as well
   Wait, I will see how heavy thou art,
(Lifts Herod a little off the ground)
   I harness a pair of rats,
(Lifts Herod higher)
   I harness a pair of cats,
(Lifts Herod still higher)

I harness a pair of mice,
(Lifts Herod upright and jumps on his back)
  Ride, devil, ride.
(Herod with the devil on his back exits upstage left)

CAPTAIN *(Comes forward looking for Herod)*
  Ah me, what hath my lord King done,
  To have slain so many a mother's son?
  Ah, had I kept myself in heed,
  My hand had never touched this deed.
  Had I this hour my will and power
  I'd hang me on the highest tree.
  Had I my power and will this hour,
  I'd drown me in the deepest sea,
  Yet I'll revenge me on my lord,
(Sits on the throne)
  And in my heart I plunge this sword.
(Plunges the sword in his heart. The lights dim quickly; there is a pause, then come up again. The Angel taps his staff on the floor, the Company and the Captain stand up; he holds the sword in front of him showing the cross of the hilt. Herod joins the Company behind Jonas. The Devil moves the throne back off stage and joins the Company as they go by in front of Herod. The Angel leads the Company anticlockwise through the Audience and back on the stage where they stand in a curve)

COMPANY *(Sing)*
  Sing, World, and shout aloud for mirth,
  Jesus, Rex, Messiah,
  He the King of Heaven and Earth,
  Natus ex Maria.
  Ox and ass the whole night through
  By the Saviour stamp and chew.
  Sing merry, sing wild,
  Sing broad, sing fine,
  Little Child,
  Thou art mine,

I am thine.
Shouting, singing, leaping springing,
Hodie,
Christ we say is born this day,
Mariae.
He with his joy
All our annoy
Away hath ta'en,
All woe, all pain.
Then make us free
To come to thee,
Make us free!
O Christe, O Christe

ANGEL *(Goes to centre of the stage, in front of the Company)*
Most reverend Worships,
(Angel shows one side of the Audience)
                    both Master
(Angel shows the other side of the Audience)
                                        and Dame,
Our service.
(Angel bows. Then showing the 'maidens' across the Audience)
            To you, pretty maidens, the same,
(Angel bows)
I come but to say, now all is ended,
We trust that in naught we have offended.
So think no evil, nor chide our play,
But if in aught we have gone astray,
And shown your Worships what was not fit,
Blame not our will,
(Lifting up and letting down his arm as in 'sorry' gesture)
                    but our lack of wit.
Think it but well, so all's made right—
And we wish you from God Almighty, Good Night.

(The Angel taps his/her staff and the Company and Angel bow to the centre, to their left and to their right. The curtain closes.

Or, the Angel goes back to fetch the Company and leads everyone anticlockwise through the Audience, singing the last song once more, and back to their places. The curtain closes when they are all still)

THE END

COLOUR PLATES

Plate 1: Paradise Play

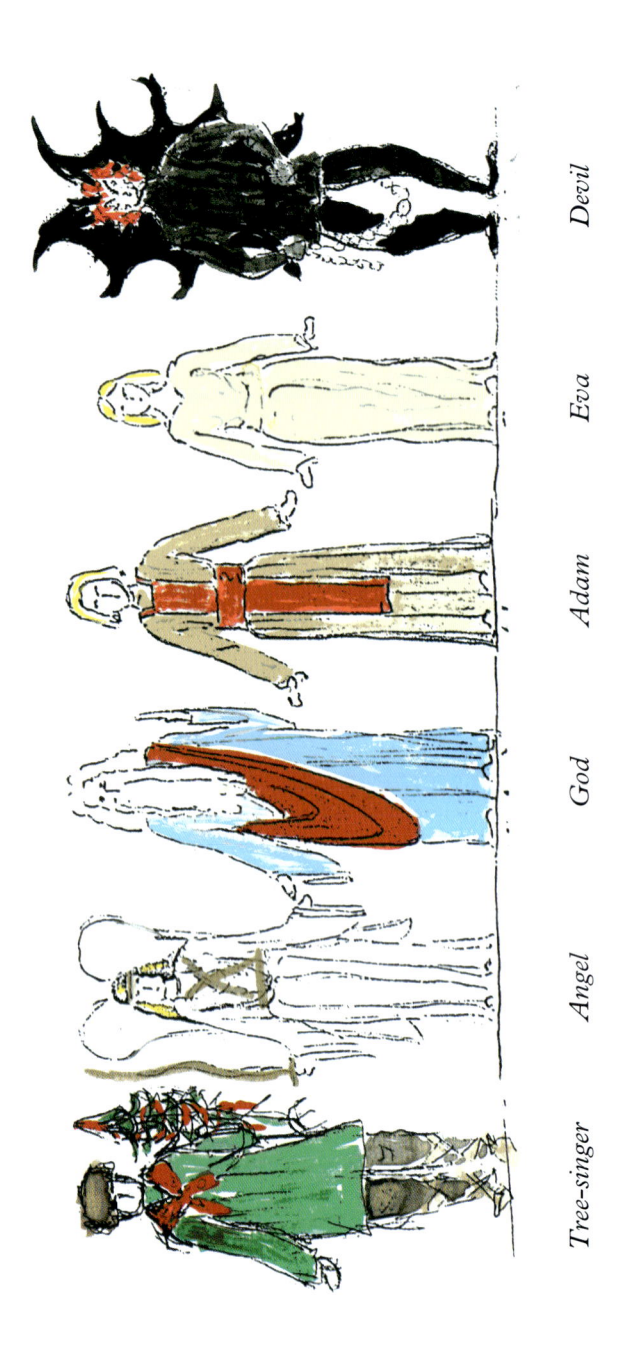

Tree-singer   Angel   God   Adam   Eva   Devil

Plate 2: Shepherds Play (1)

Angel   Mary   Joseph   Star-singer

Plate 3: Shepherds Play (2)

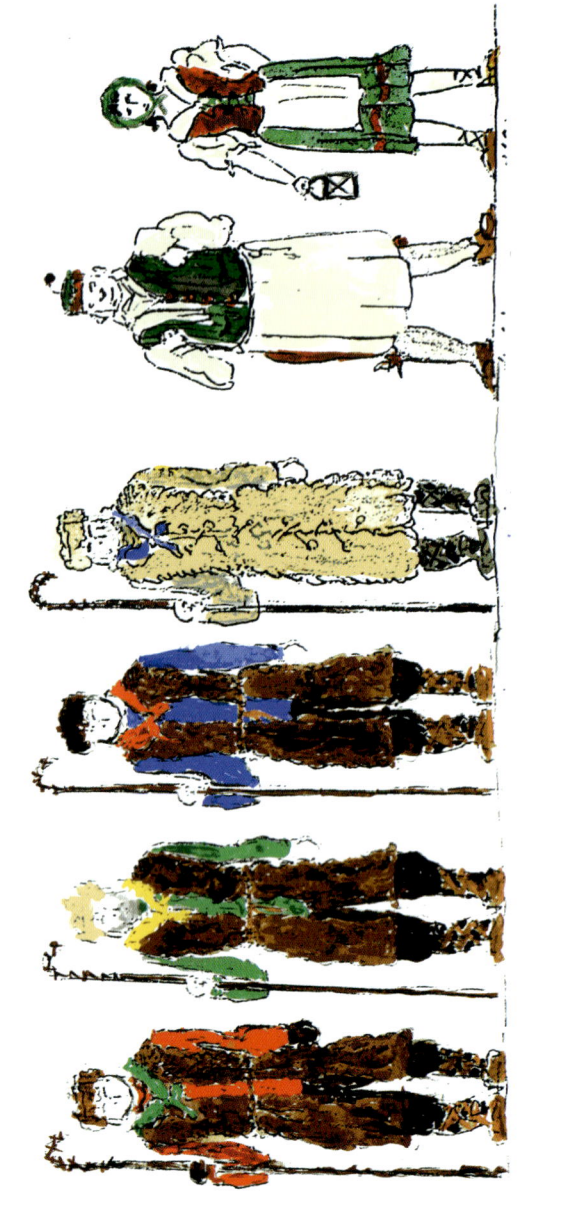

Huckle   Muckle   Gallus   Crispin   Innkeepers

Plate 4: Kings Play (1)

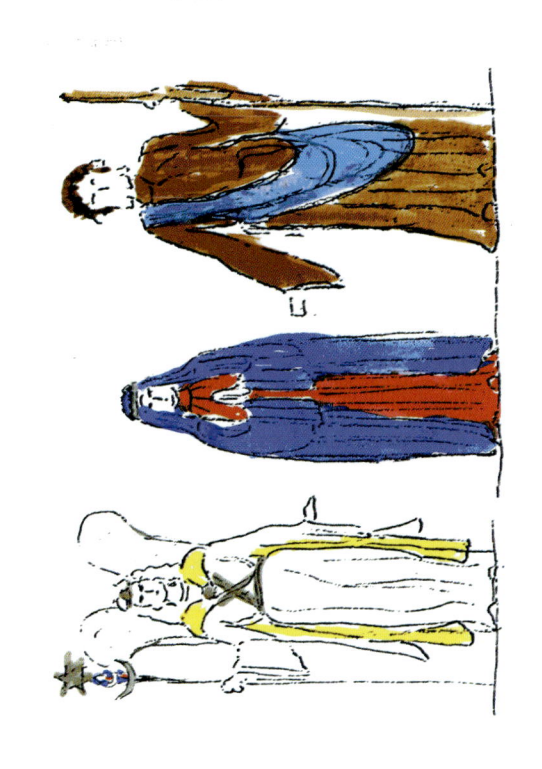

Angel   *Mary*   *Joseph*

Plate 5: Kings Play (2)

Caspar   Melchior   Balthazzar   Page   Viligratia   Judas